EASY GUITAR WITH NOTES & TAB

THE ESSENTIAL

BOB MARLEY

Photo courtesy of Bob Marley Music, Inc.

ISBN 978-0-634-04739-8

HAL•LEONARD®
CORPORATION
7777 W. BLUEMOUND RD. P.O. BOX 13819 MILWAUKEE, WI 53213

Visit Hal Leonard Online at
www.halleonard.com

USING THE STRUM PATTERNS

The songs in this book include suggested strum patterns (Strum Pattern 1.) for guitar. These numbers refer to the numbered strum patterns below.

The strumming notation uses special symbols to indicate up and down strokes.

$$\sqcap = \text{DOWN}$$

$$\vee = \text{UP}$$

Feel free to experiment with these basic patterns to create your own rhythmic accompaniment.

STRUM PATTERNS

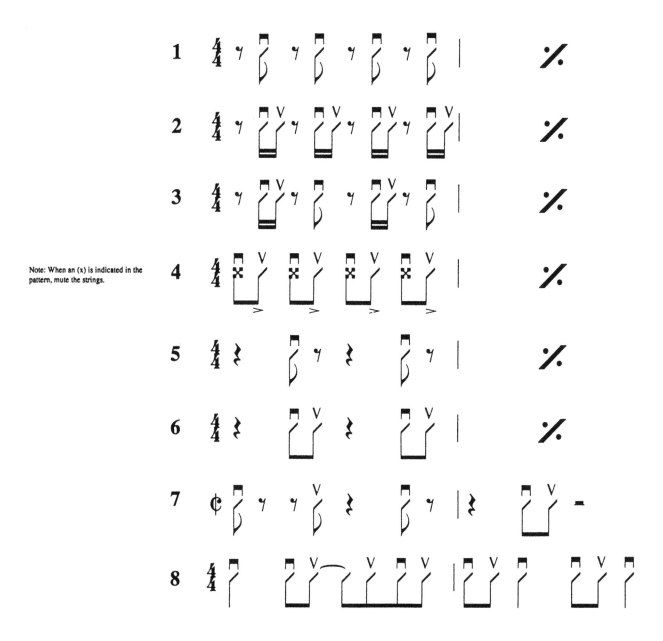

Note: When an (x) is indicated in the pattern, mute the strings.

Africa Unite

Words and Music by Bob Marley

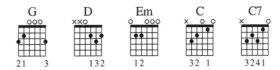

Strum Pattern: 5, 6

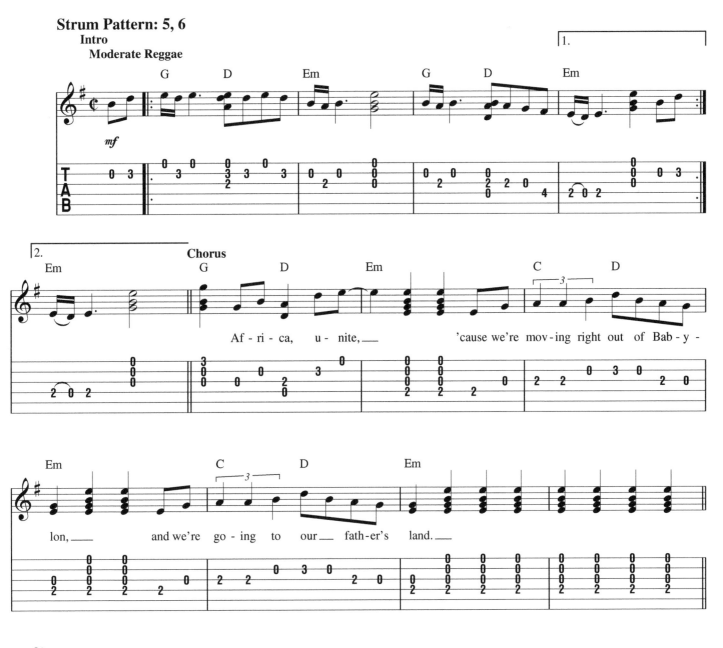

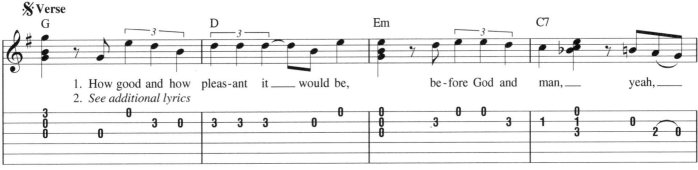

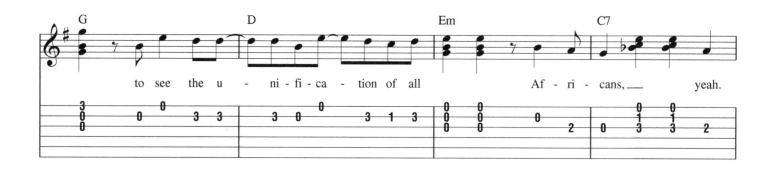

to see the u - ni - fi - ca - tion of all Af - ri - cans, ___ yeah.

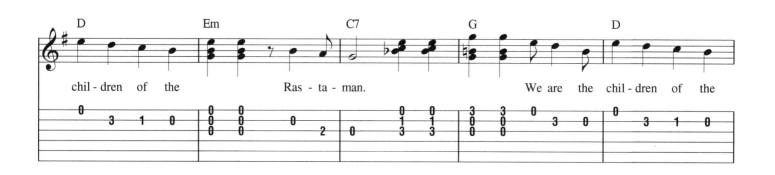

As it's been said al-read-y, let it be done, yeah. We are the

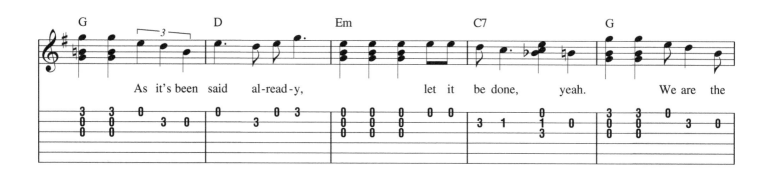

chil - dren of the Ras - ta - man. We are the chil - dren of the

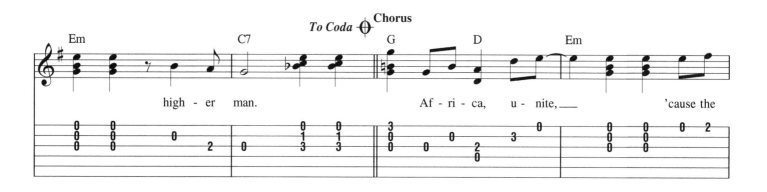

To Coda ⊕ **Chorus**

high - er man. Af - ri - ca, u - nite, ___ 'cause the

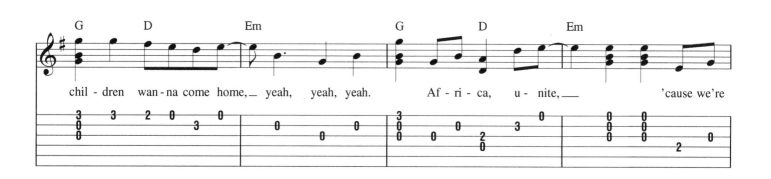

chil - dren wan - na come home, ___ yeah, yeah, yeah. Af - ri - ca, u - nite, ___ 'cause we're

moving right out of Bab-y - lon, __ and we're groov-ing to our __ fath-er's land. __

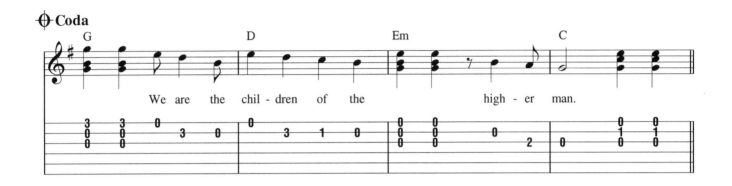

Coda

We are the chil - dren of the high - er man.

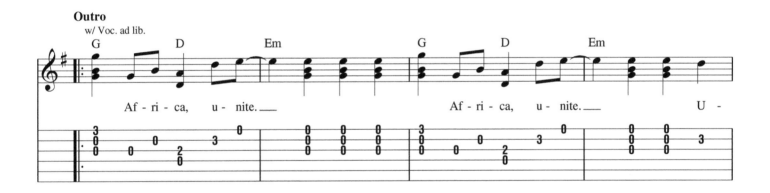

Outro
w/ Voc. ad lib.

Af - ri - ca, u - nite. __ Af - ri - ca, u - nite. __ U -

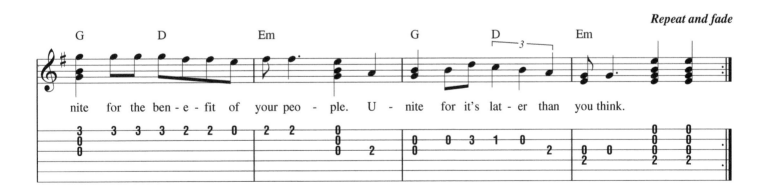

Repeat and fade

nite for the ben - e - fit of your peo - ple. U - nite for it's lat - er than you think.

Additional Lyrics

2. How good and how pleasant it would be,
   Before God and man,
   To see the unification of all Rastaman, yeah.
   As it's been said already, let it be done, yeah.
   I tell you who we are under the sun.
   We are the children of the Rastaman.
   We are the children of the higher man.

Buffalo Soldier

Words and Music by Noel Williams and Bob Marley

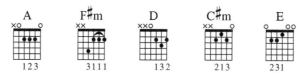

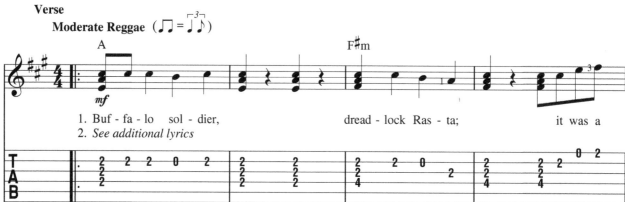

Strum Pattern: 5

Verse

Moderate Reggae

1. Buf - fa - lo sol - dier, dread - lock Ras - ta; it was a
2. *See additional lyrics*

buf - fa - lo sol - dier in the heart of A - mer - i - ca.

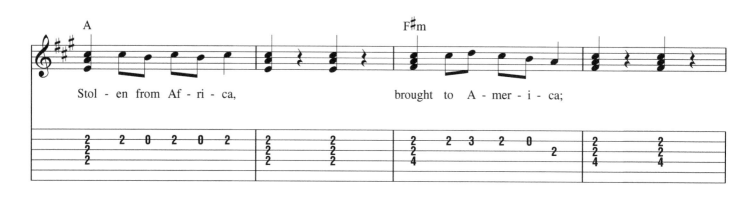

Stol - en from Af - ri - ca, brought to A - mer - i - ca;

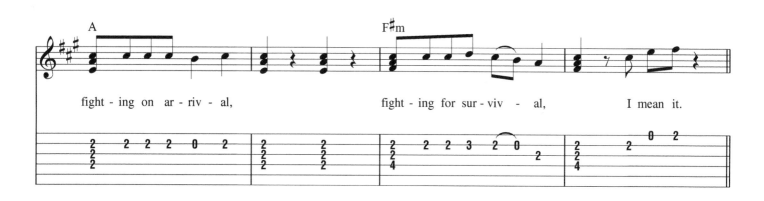

fight - ing on ar - riv - al, fight - ing for sur - viv - al, I mean it.

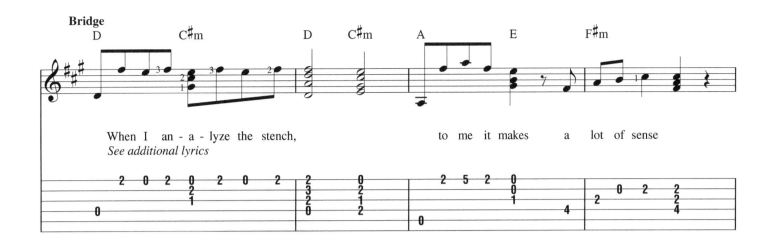

Bridge

When I an - a - lyze the stench, to me it makes a lot of sense
See additional lyrics

how the dread - lock Ras - ta was the buf - fa - lo sol - dier. 2. And he was

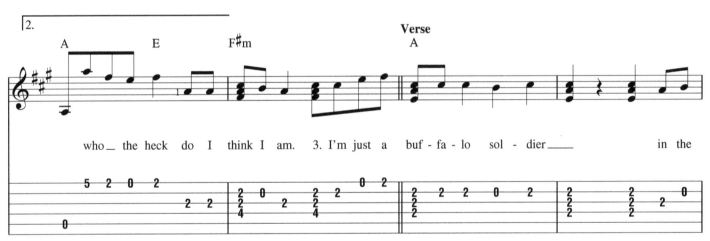

who __ the heck do I think I am. 3. I'm just a buf - fa - lo sol - dier ____ in the

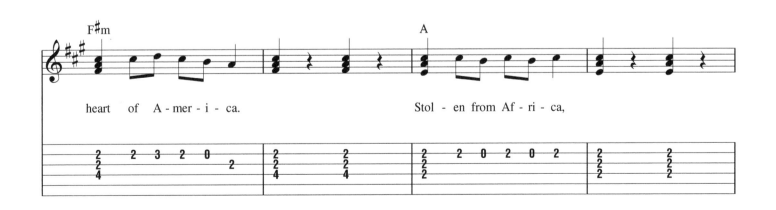

heart of A - mer - i - ca. Stol - en from Af - ri - ca,

9

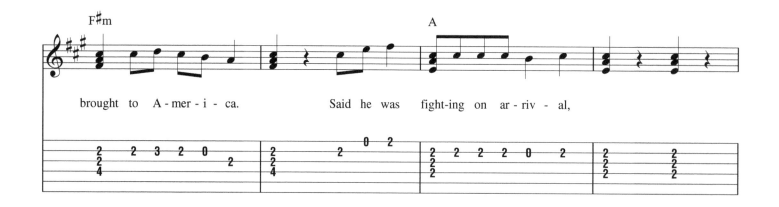

brought to A-mer-i-ca. Said he was fight-ing on ar-riv-al,

fight-ing for sur-viv-al._____ Said he was the buf-fa-lo sol-dier, in the

war for A-mer-i-ca. Sing-ing: Wo, yo, yo, wo,___ yo, yo, yo.

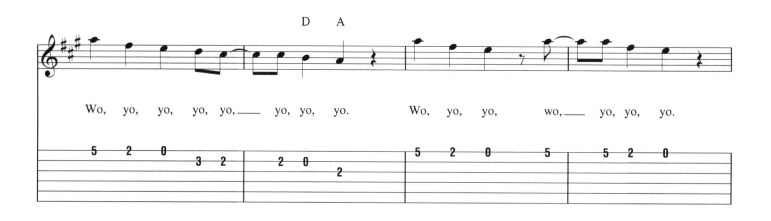

Wo, yo, yo, yo, yo,___ yo, yo, yo. Wo, yo, yo, wo,___ yo, yo, yo.

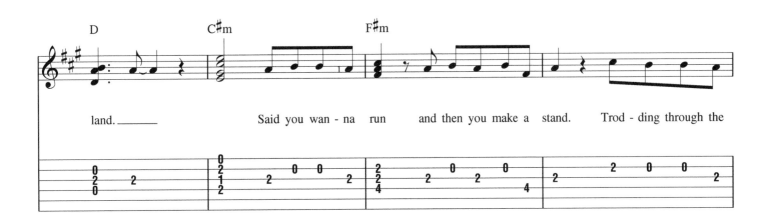

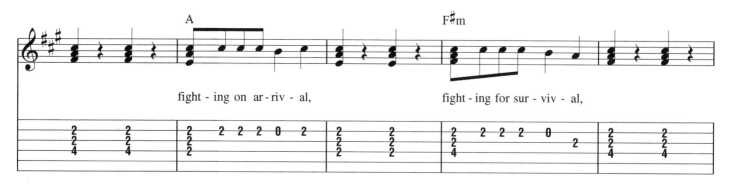

fight - ing on ar - riv - al,   fight - ing for sur - viv - al,

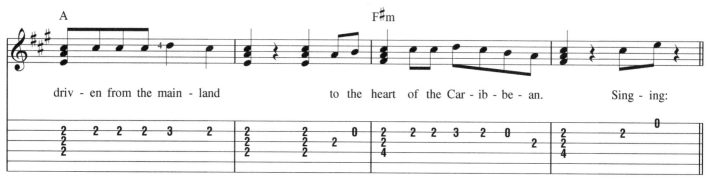

driv - en from the main - land   to the heart of the Car - ib - be - an.   Sing - ing:

Outro

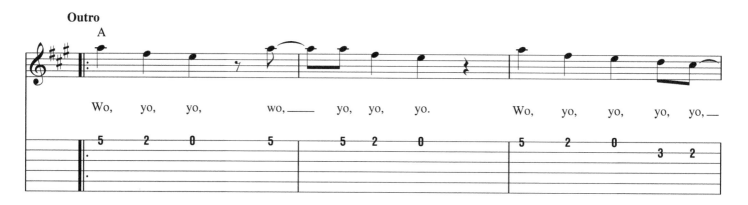

Wo,   yo,   yo,   wo,___ yo,   yo,   yo.   Wo,   yo,   yo,   yo,   yo,___

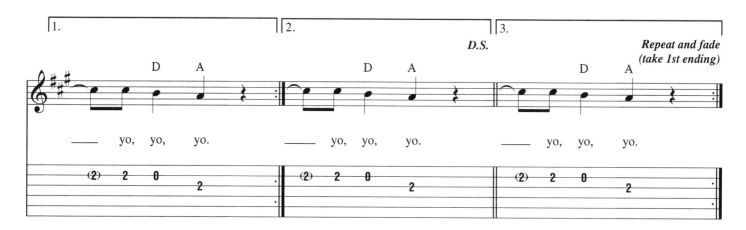

|1. |2. |3.

D.S.   *Repeat and fade (take 1st ending)*

___ yo,   yo,   yo.   ___ yo,   yo,   yo.   ___ yo,   yo,   yo.

Additional Lyrics

2. And he was taken from Africa, brought to America,
   Fighting on arrival, fighting for survival.
   Said he was a buffalo soldier, dreadlock Rasta,
   Buffalo soldier in the heart of America.

Bridge If you know your history,
   Then you would know where you're coming from.
   Then you wouldn't have to ask me
   Who the heck do I think I am.

5. Trodding through San Juan in the arms of America.
   Trodding through Jamaica, the buffalo soldier.
   Fighting on arrival, fighting for survival.
   Buffalo soldier, dreadlock Rasta.

Could You Be Loved

Words and Music by Bob Marley

Strum Pattern: 1

Intro

Moderately bright Reggae

Chorus

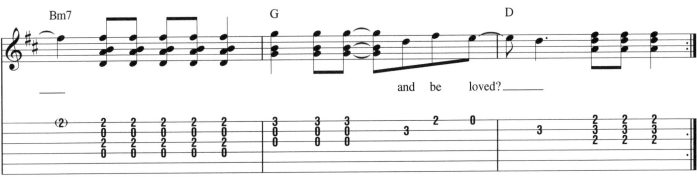

Could you be loved

and be loved?

Verse

1. Don't let them fool you
2. *See additional lyrics*

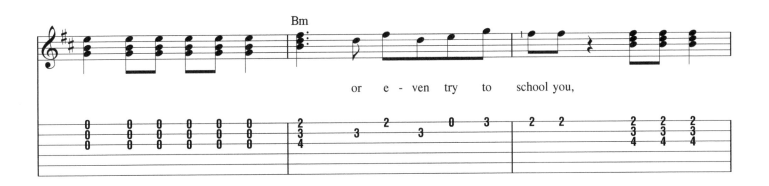

or e - ven try to school you,

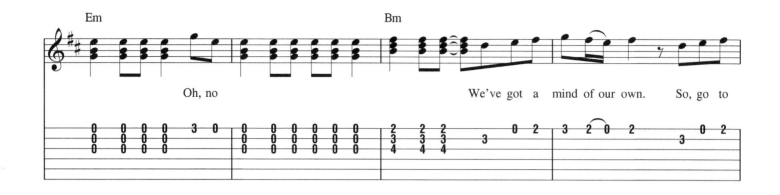

Oh, no ... We've got a mind of our own. So, go to

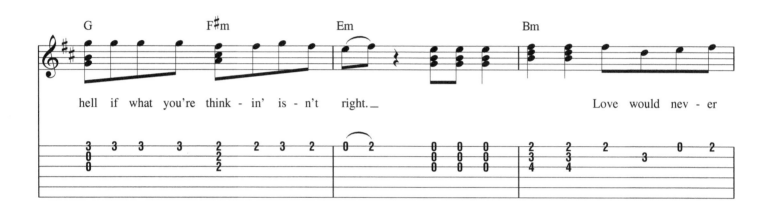

hell if what you're think - in' is - n't right. ___ Love would nev - er

To Coda ⊕

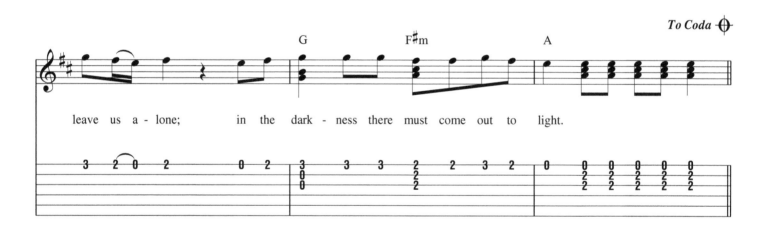

leave us a - lone; in the dark - ness there must come out to light.

Chorus

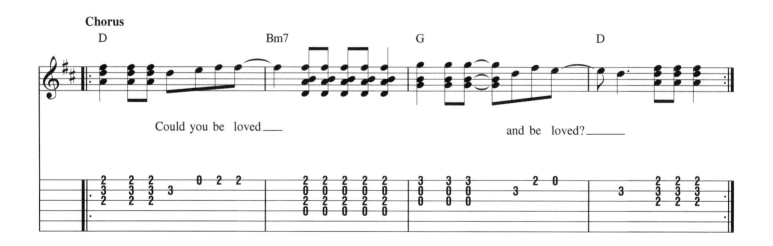

Could you be loved ___ and be loved? ___

Interlude

The road of life is rock - y and you may stum - ble too. So

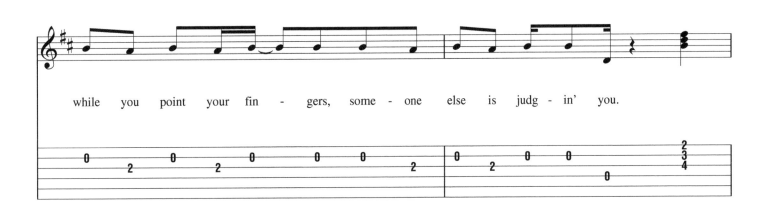

while you point your fin - gers, some - one else is judg - in' you.

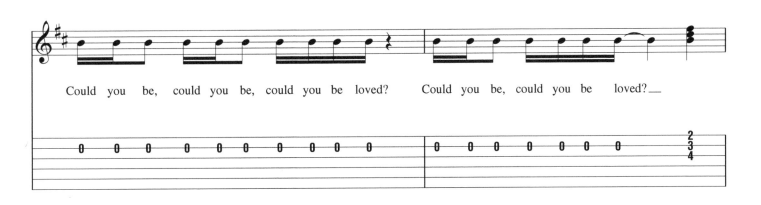

Could you be, could you be, could you be loved? Could you be, could you be loved?___

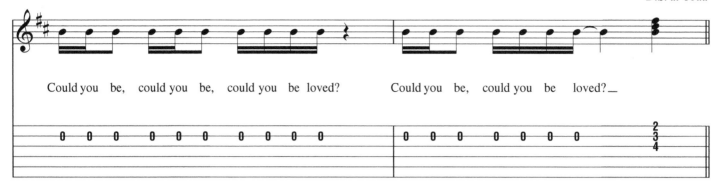

Could you be, could you be, could you be loved? Could you be, could you be loved?___

⊕ Coda

Chorus

Stay a - live,___ oh. Could you be loved___

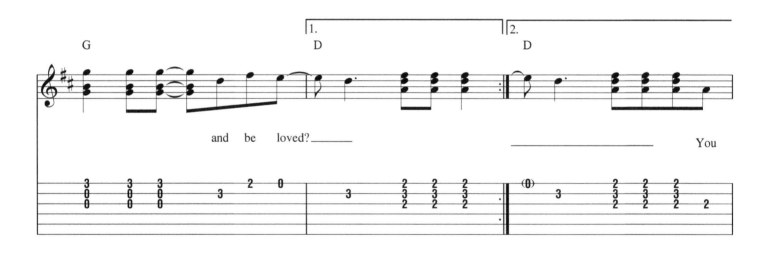

and be loved?_____ You

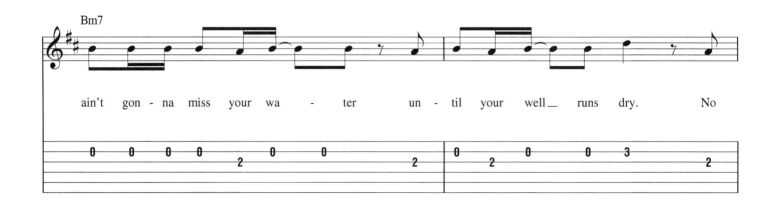

ain't gon - na miss your wa - ter un - til your well___ runs dry. No

mat - ter how __ you treat him, the man will nev - er be sat - is - fied.

Could you be, could you be, could you be loved?   Could you be, could you be be loved?

Repeat and fade

Outro
w/ Voc. ad lib.
Bm

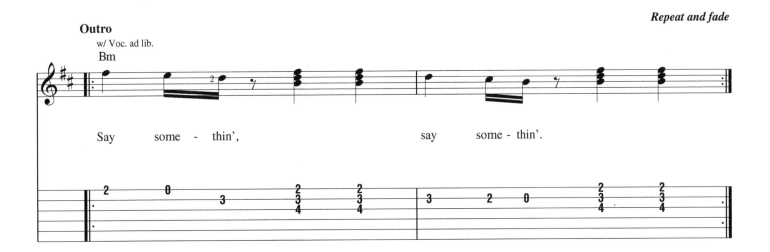

Say   some - thin',   say   some - thin'.

Additional Lyrics

2. Don't let them change you
   Or even rearrange you, oh, no.
   We've got a life to live.
   They say only, only, only the
   Fittest of the fittest shall survive.
   Stay alive, oh.

Crazy Baldhead

Words and Music by Rita Marley and Vincent Ford

Strum Pattern: 5

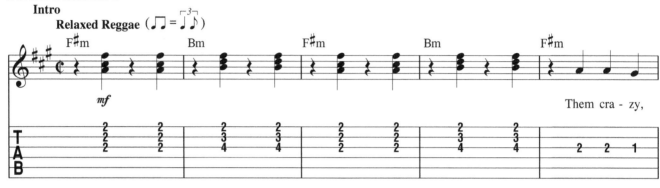

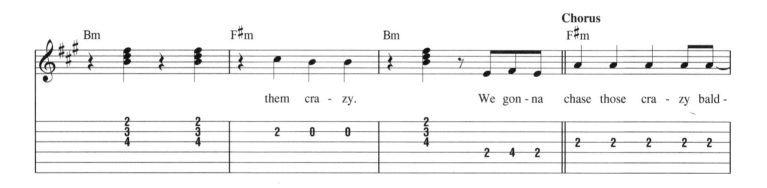

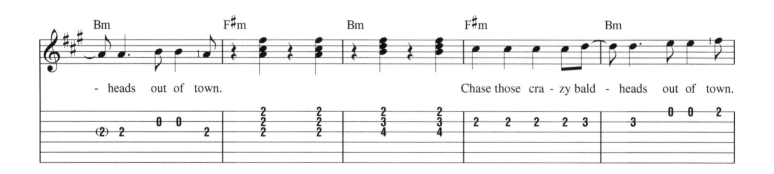

1. I and I build the cab - in,
2. *See additional lyrics*

I and I plant the corn. ___ Did -n't my peo -ple be - fore me

slave for this coun - try? ___ Now you look me with a scorn, ___ then you

Chorus

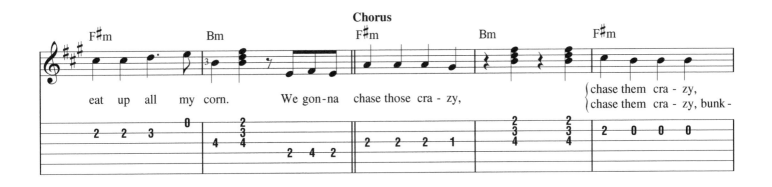

eat up all my corn. We gon-na chase those cra - zy, { chase them cra - zy,
{ chase them cra - zy, bunk -

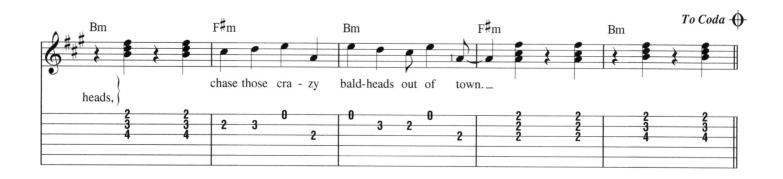

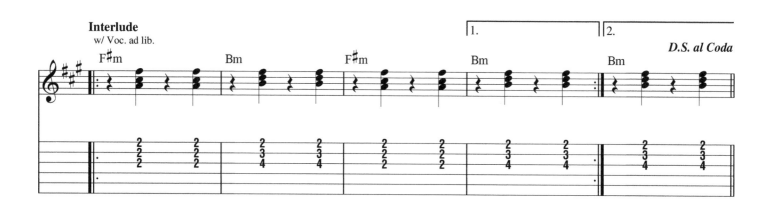

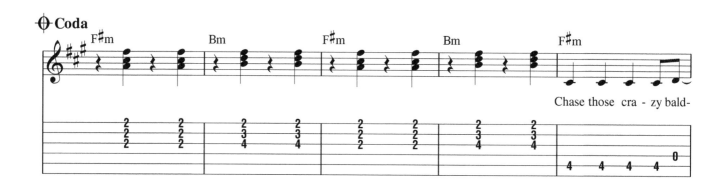

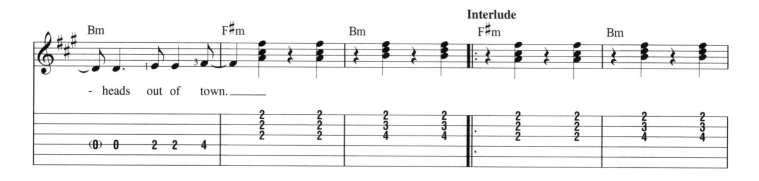

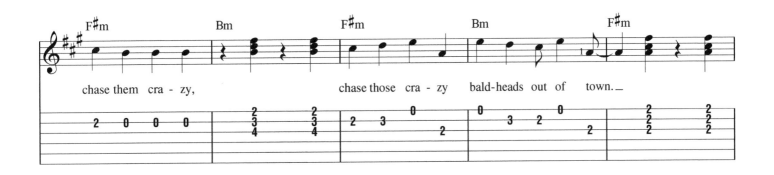

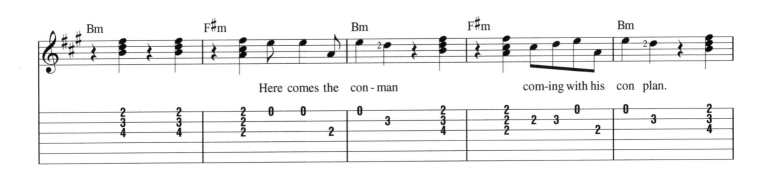

Additional Lyrics

2. Build your penitentiary, we build your schools.
Brainwash education to make us the fools.
Hate is your reward for our love
Telling us of your God above.

Get Up Stand Up

Words and Music by Bob Marley and Peter Tosh

Am

Strum Pattern: 6

Intro

Moderately slow Reggae

Chorus

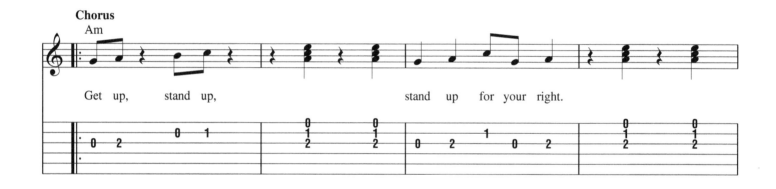

Get up,   stand up,   stand up   for your right.

Get up,   stand up,

{ 1. stand   up   for your right. }
{ 2., 3. don't   give   up   the fight. }

Get up,   stand up,   don't give   up the fight.

Verse

1. Preach - er man, don't tell me ___ heav - en is un - der the earth. ___
2., 3. *See additional lyrics*

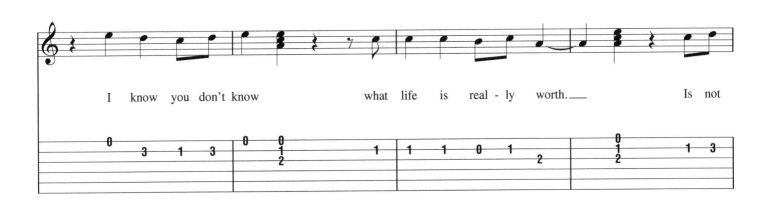

I know you don't know what life is real - ly worth. ___ Is not

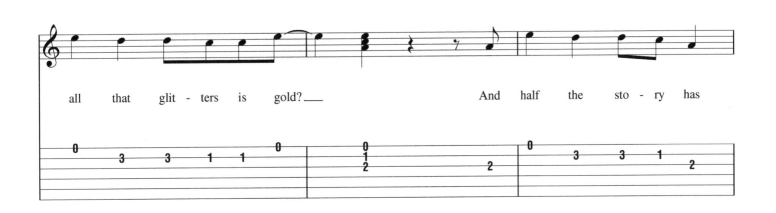

all that glit - ters is gold? ___ And half the sto - ry has

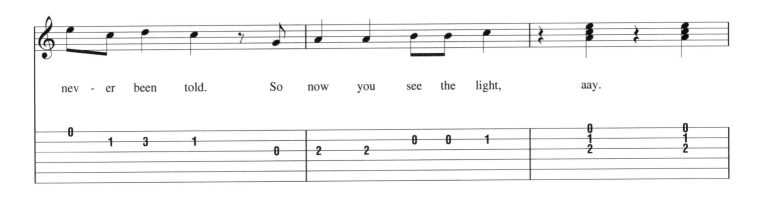

nev - er been told. So now you see the light, aay.

Stand up for your right.___ Come on, Stand up for your right. So you'd bet - ter

Outro-Chorus

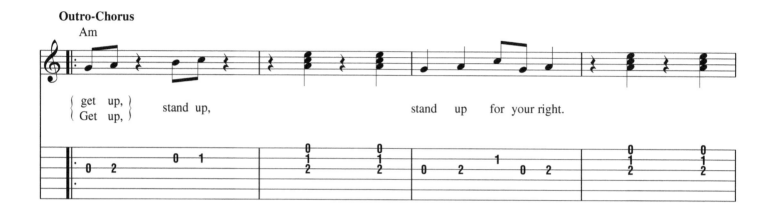

{ get up, } stand up, stand up for your right.
{ Get up, }

Repeat and fade

Get up, stand up, don't give up the fight.

Additional Lyrics

2. Most people think great God will come from the sky,
   Take away ev'rything, and make ev'rybody feel high.
   But if you know what life is worth,
   You would look for yours on earth.
   And now you see the light.
   You stand up for your right, yah!

3. We're sick and tired of your ism and skism game.
   Die and go to heaven in Jesus' name, Lord.
   We know when we understand. Almighty God is a living man.
   You can fool some people sometimes,
   But you can't fool all the people all the time.
   So now we see the light. We gonna stand up for our right.

Guava Jelly

Words and Music by Bob Marley

Strum Pattern: 2

Intro
Moderate Reggae

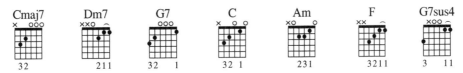

1. You said you love me. _____ I said I

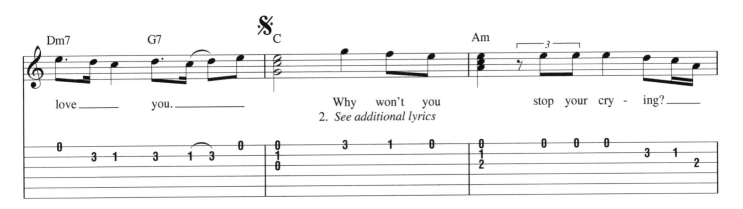

love _____ you. _____ Why won't you stop your cry - ing? _____

2. *See additional lyrics*

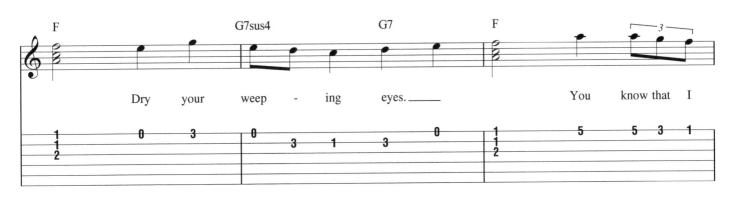

Dry your weep - ing eyes. _____ You know that I

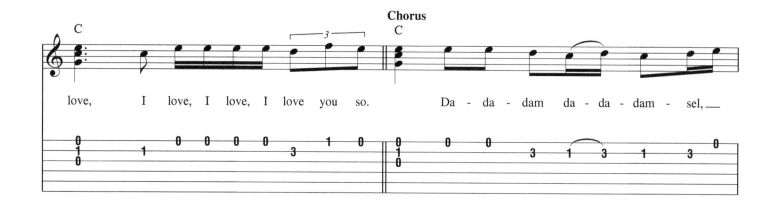

love, I love, I love, I love you so. Da - da - dam da - da - dam - sel, ___

here I am. ___ Me said, "Come rub it 'pon me bel - ly with you

gua - va jel - ly." Da - da - da da - da - dam - sel, here I stand. ___ Come ___

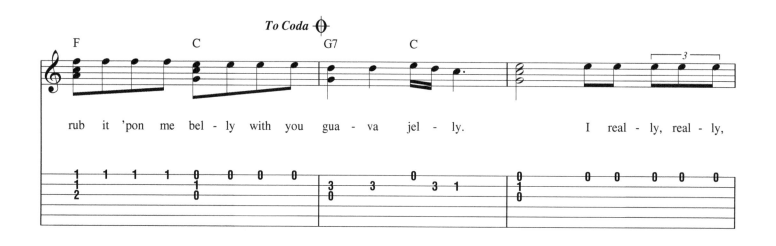

rub it 'pon me bel - ly with you gua - va jel - ly. I real - ly, real - ly,

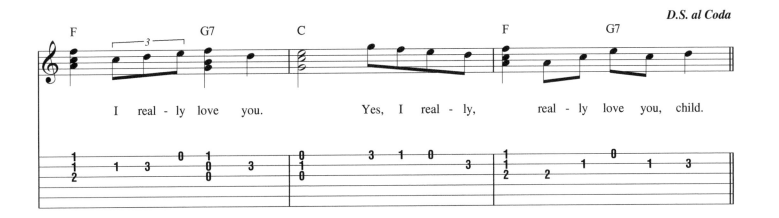

Repeat and fade

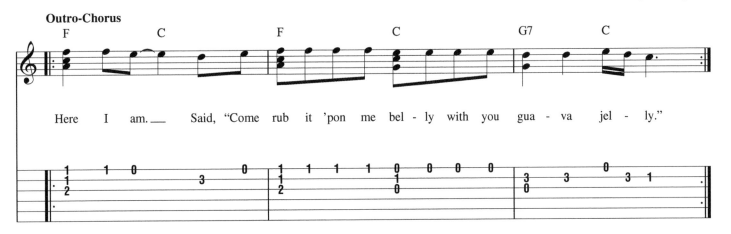

Additional Lyrics

2. I'll say you should stop, stop crying.
   Wipe your weeping eyes.
   You'll see how I'm gonna love,
   Love you from the bottom of my heart.

I Shot the Sheriff

Words and Music by Bob Marley

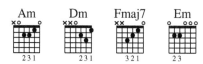

Strum Pattern: 3

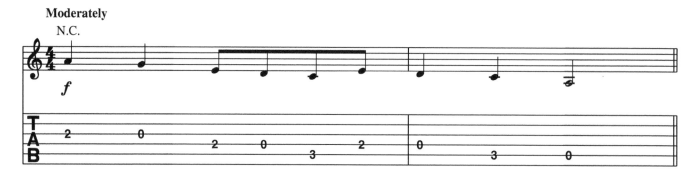

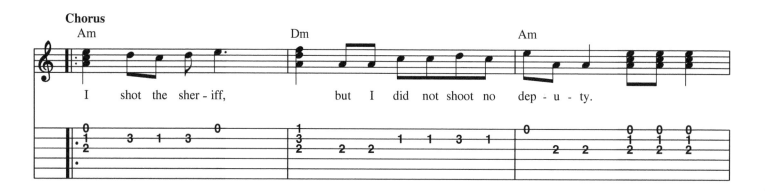

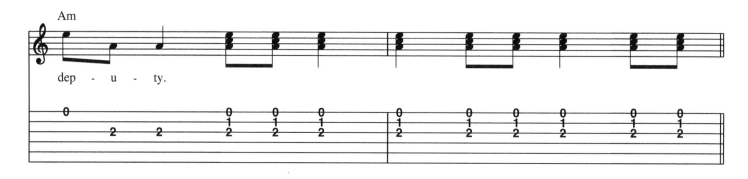

Additional Lyrics

2. Sheriff John Brown always hated me;
   For what, I don't know.
   And every time that I plant a seed,
   He said, "Kill it before it grows,"
   "Kill it before it grows."

3. Freedom came our way one day,
   So I started out of town.
   All of a sudden, I see Sheriff Brown
   Aimin' to shoot me down,
   So I shot him down.

4. Reflexes got the better of me,
   What will be will be.
   Every day, the bucket goes to the well,
   One day the bottom will drop out
   I say, one day the bottom will drop out.

Iron Lion Zion

Words and Music by Bob Marley

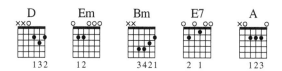

Strum Pattern: 6

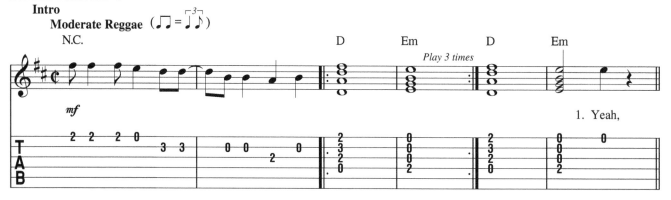

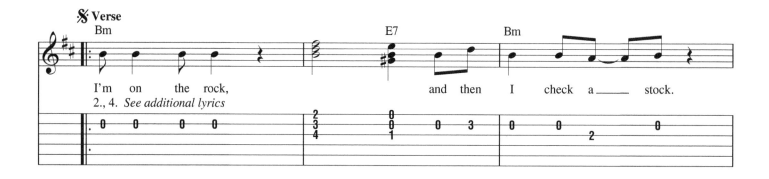

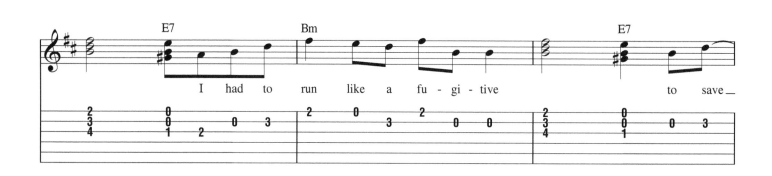

____ the life I live. I'm gon - na be i - ron like a_

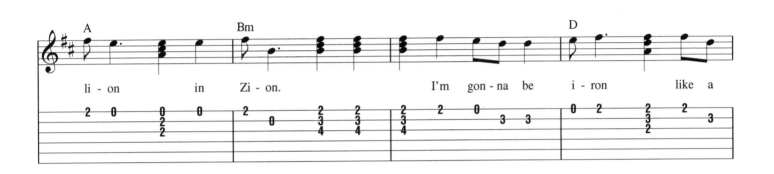

li - on in Zi - on. I'm gon - na be i - ron like a

Chorus

_li - on in Zi - on._

To Coda

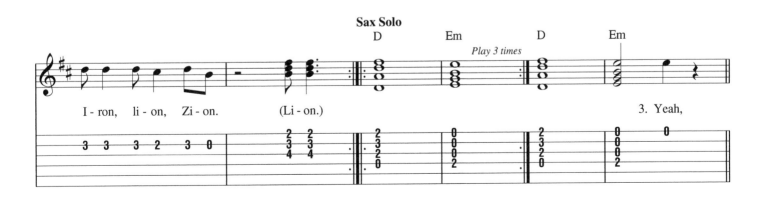

Sax Solo

I - ron, li - on, Zi - on. (Li - on.)   _3. Yeah,_

Play 3 times

Verse

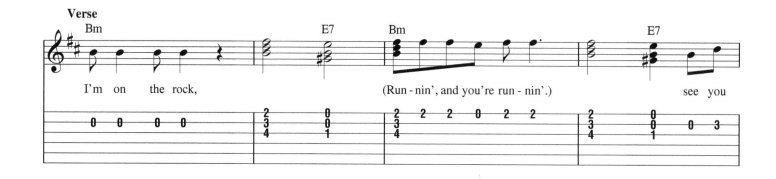

I'm on the rock, (Run - nin', and you're run - nin'.) see you

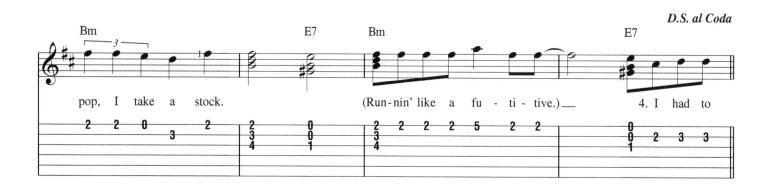

D.S. al Coda

pop, I take a stock. (Run - nin' like a fu - ti - tive.) 4. I had to

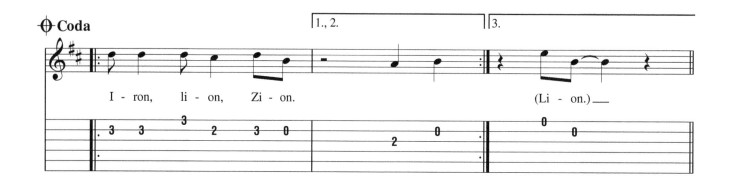

Coda

I - ron, li - on, Zi - on. (Li - on.)

Outro

Repeat and fade

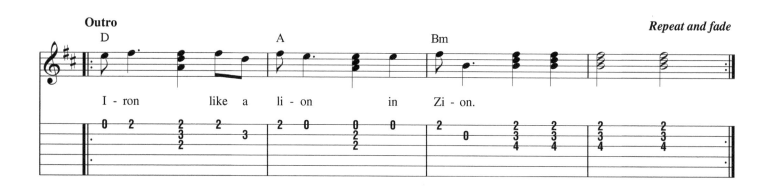

I - ron like a li - on in Zi - on.

Additional Lyrics

2. I'm on the run, but I ain't got no gun.
   See, they want to be the star,
   So they fighting tribal war.
   And they saying...

4. I had to run like a fugitive,
   Ooh God, just to, just to save the life I live.
   Oh now, I'm gonna be...

Is This Love

Words and Music by Bob Marley

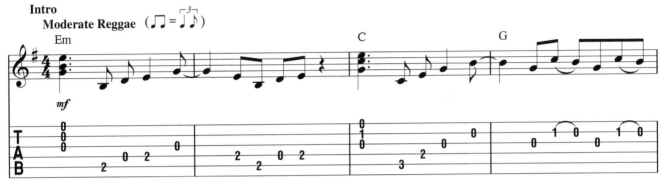

Strum Pattern: 5

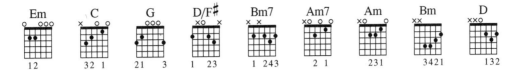

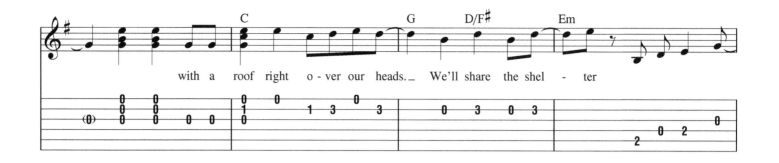

with a   roof   right   o - ver   our   heads.__ We'll   share   the   shel   -   ter

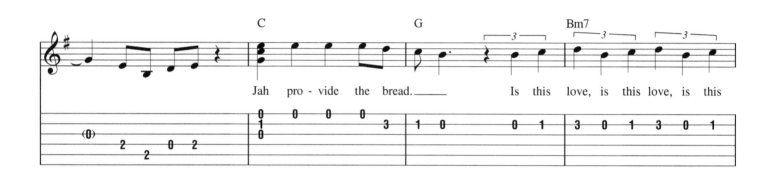

of   my   sin - gle   bed.__ We'll   share   the   same __ room,

Jah   pro - vide   the   bread._____ Is   this   love,   is   this   love,   is   this

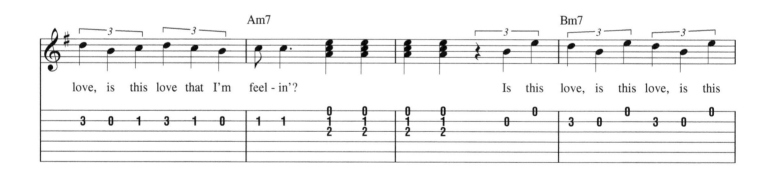

love,   is   this   love   that   I'm   feel - in'?   Is   this   love,   is   this   love,   is   this

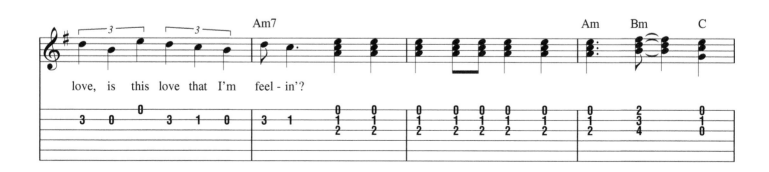

love,   is   this   love   that   I'm   feel - in'?

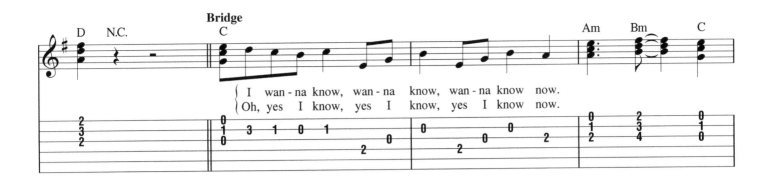

I wan-na know, wan-na know, wan-na know now.
Oh, yes I know, yes I know, yes I know now.

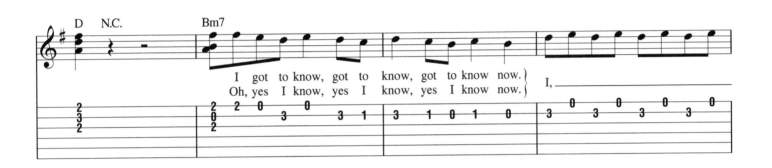

I got to know, got to know, got to know now.
Oh, yes I know, yes I know, yes I know now.

I,

I'm will-ing and a - ble,

so I   throw my

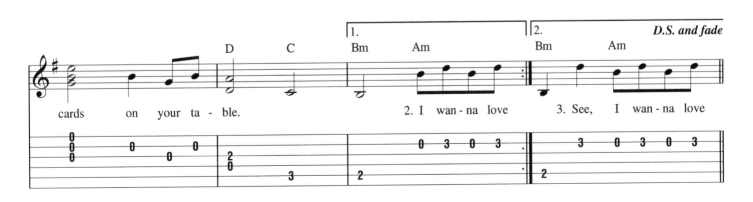

cards   on   your ta - ble.

2. I wan-na love

3. See, I wan-na love

Jamming

Words and Music by Bob Marley

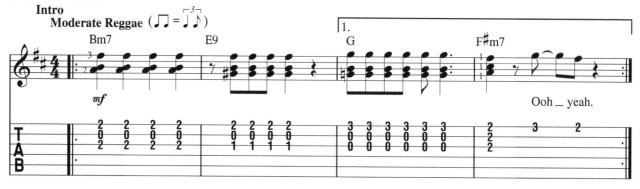

Strum Pattern: 4

Intro
Moderate Reggae

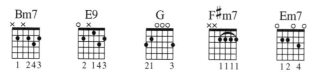

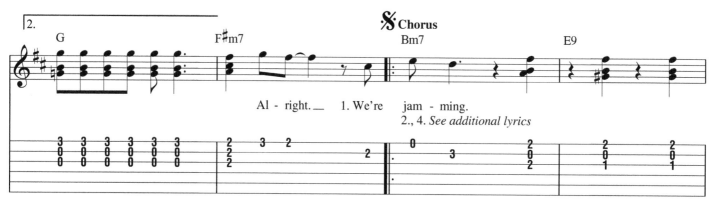

Ooh _ yeah.

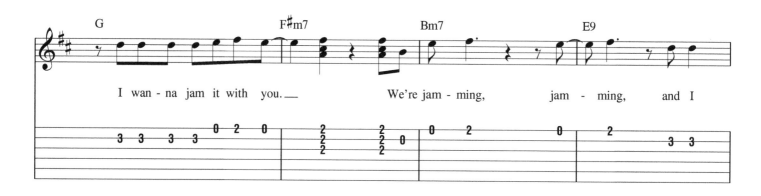

Chorus

Al - right. __ 1. We're jam - ming.
2., 4. *See additional lyrics*

I wan - na jam it with you. __   We're jam - ming, jam - ming, and I

Verse

hope you like jam - ming, too. __   1. Ain't no rules, __ ain't no vow, __ we can do
2., 3. *See additional lyrics*

it an - y how.___ I and I will see you through.___ 'Cause ev - er - y

To Coda ⊕

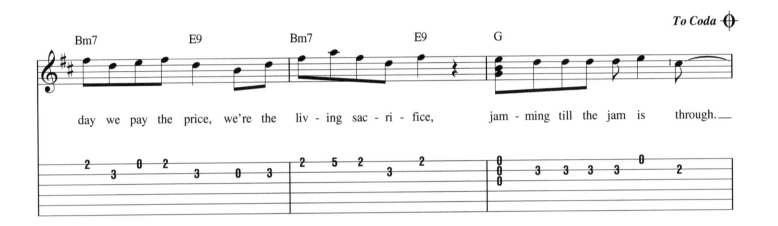

day we pay the price, we're the liv - ing sac - ri - fice, jam - ming till the jam is through.___

___ 2. We're ___ 3. We're jam - ming, (Jam - ming, jam - ming, jam - ming.) and we're

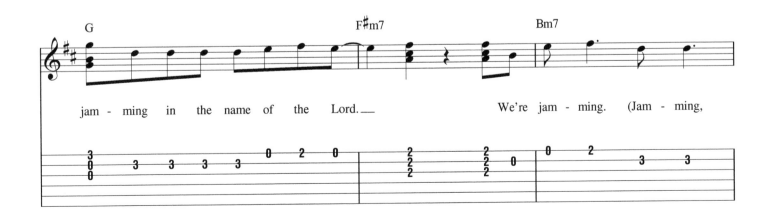

jam - ming in the name of the Lord.___ We're jam - ming. (Jam - ming,

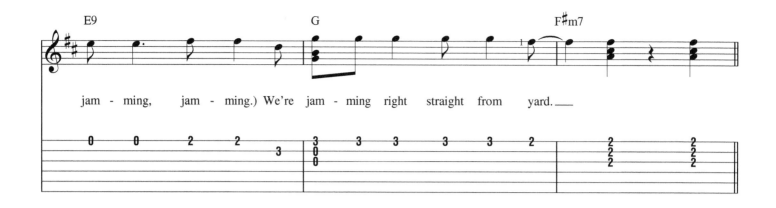

jam - ming, jam - ming.) We're jam - ming right straight from yard. __

Interlude

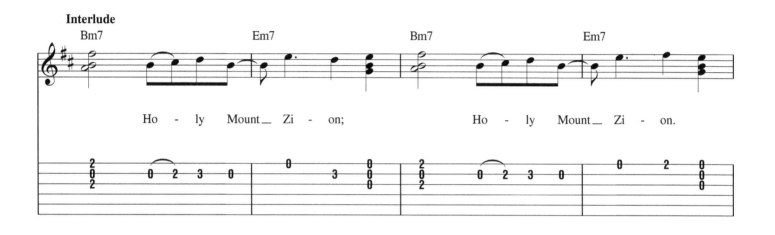

Ho - ly Mount __ Zi - on; Ho - ly Mount __ Zi - on.

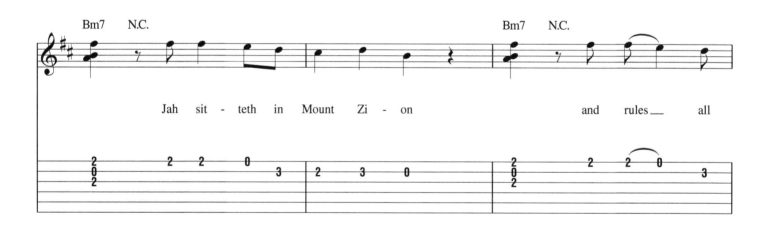

Jah sit - teth in Mount Zi - on and rules __ all

D.S. al Coda

cre - a - tion. Yeah, we're, we're jam - ming. 4. Bop - chu - wa - wa -

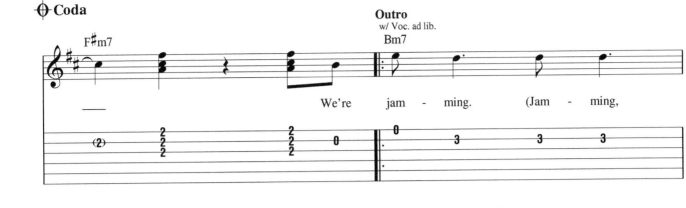

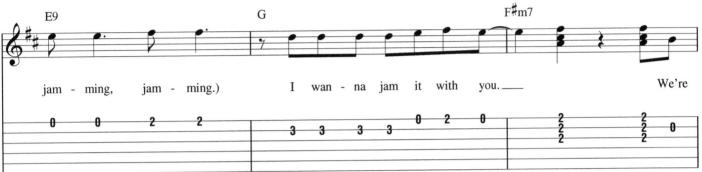

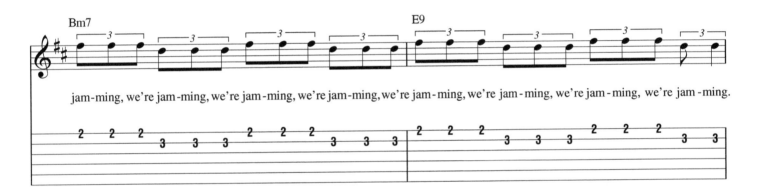

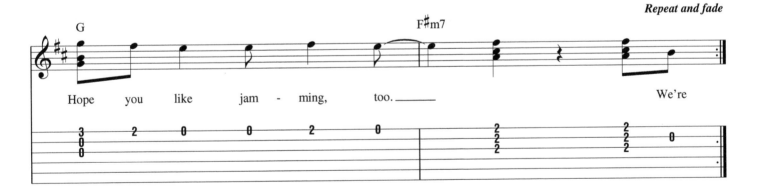

Additional Lyrics

Chorus 2. We're jamming.
    To think that jamming was a thing of the past.
    We're jamming,
    And I hope this jam is gonna last.

  2. No bullet can stop us now, we neither beg nor we won't bow,
    Neither can be bought nor sold.
    We all defend the right, Jah Jah children must unite,
    For life is worth much more than gold.

Chorus 4. Bop-chu-wa-wa-wa. We're jamming.
    I wanna jam it with you.
    We're jamming,
    And jam down, hope your jamming, too.

  3. Jah knows how much I've tried, the truth cannot hide,
    To keep you satisfied.
    True love that now exists is the love I can't resist,
    So jam by my side.

Lively Up Yourself

Words and Music by Bob Marley

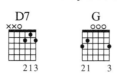

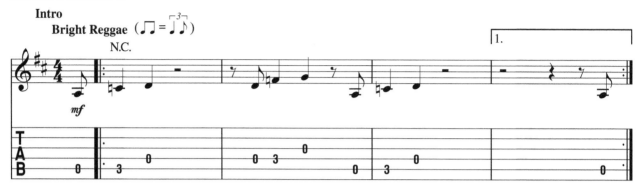

Strum Pattern: 6

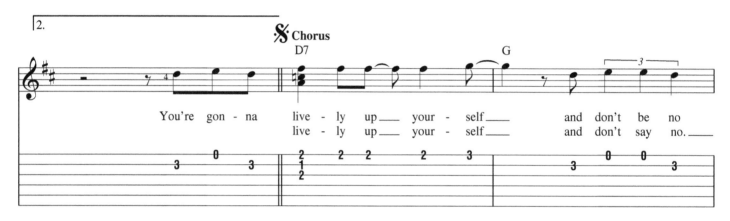

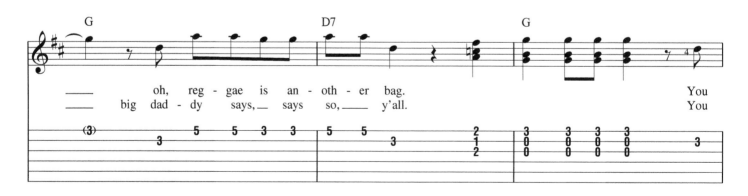

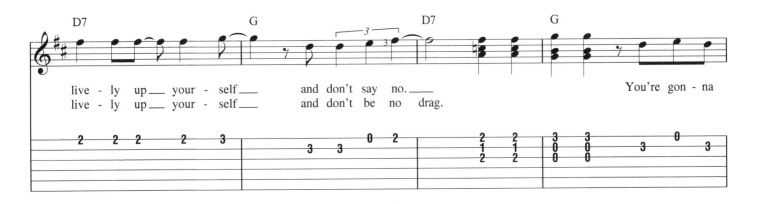

live - ly up___ your - self___ and don't say no.___ You're gon - na
live - ly up___ your - self___ and don't be no drag.

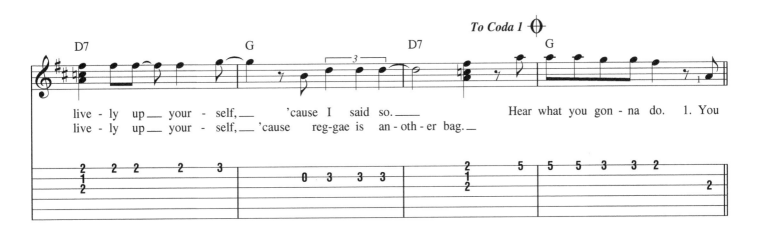

To Coda 1

live - ly up___ your - self,___ 'cause I said so.___ Hear what you gon - na do. 1. You
live - ly up___ your - self,___ 'cause reg-gae is an - oth - er bag.___

Verse

rock so you rock so, like you nev - er did be - fore. You
rock so you rock so. You

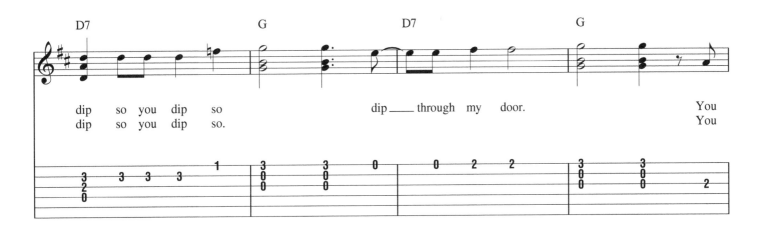

dip so you dip so dip___ through my door. You
dip so you dip so. You

come so you come so. Oh,___ yeah. You
skank so you skank so, and don't be no drag. You

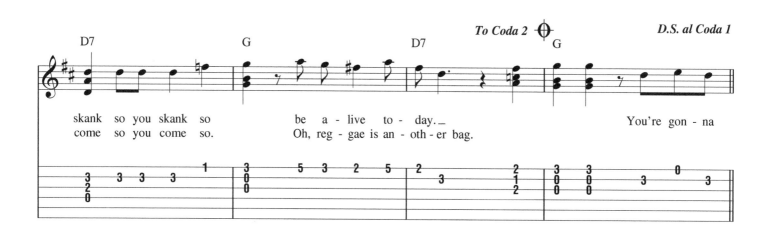

To Coda 2 𝄌 *D.S. al Coda 1*

skank so you skank so be a - live to - day.___ You're gon - na
come so you come so. Oh, reg - gae is an - oth - er bag. You're gon - na

𝄌 **Coda 1**

Verse

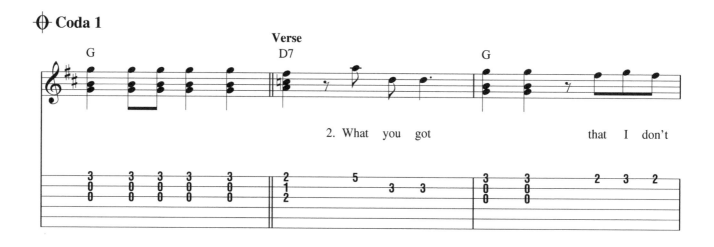

2. What you got that I don't

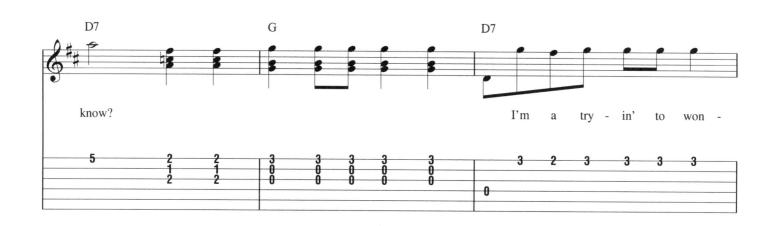

know? I'm a try - in' to won -

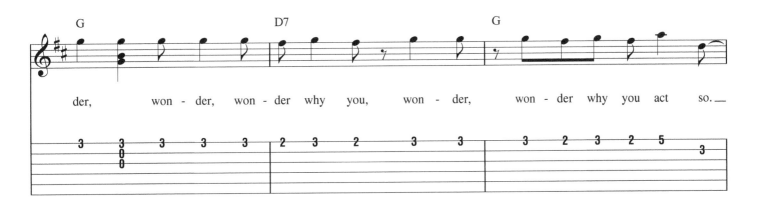

der,   won - der,   won - der why you,   won - der,   won - der why you act   so. —

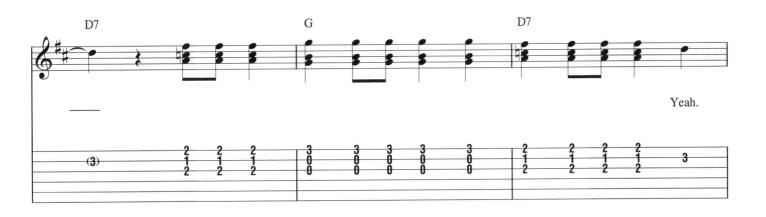

— Yeah.

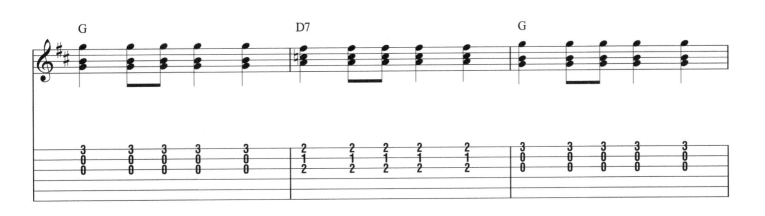

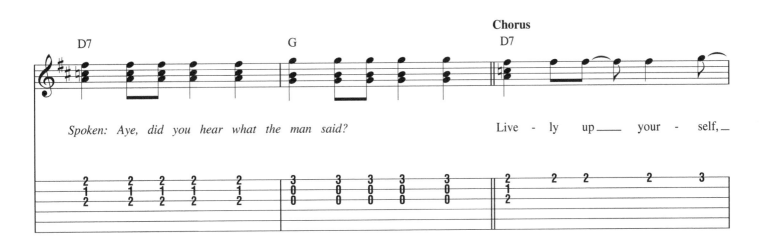

Chorus

Spoken: Aye, did you hear what the man said?   Live - ly   up — your - self, —

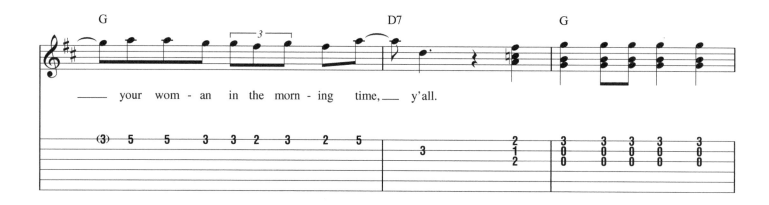

your wom - an in the morn - ing time, ___ y'all.

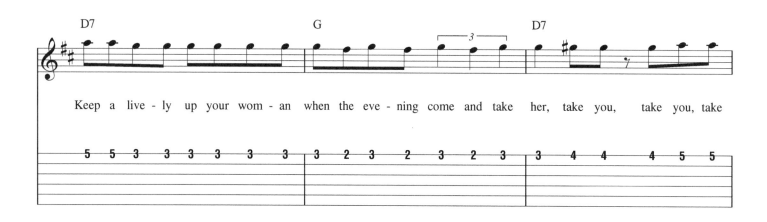

Keep a live - ly up your wom - an when the eve - ning come and take her, take you, take you, take

Interlude

you. ___ Come on, ___ ba - by, 'cause I, I wan - na be

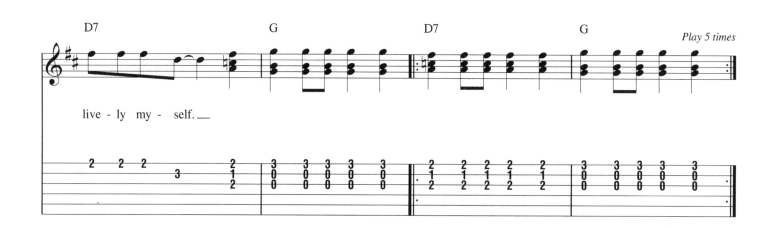

Play 5 times

live - ly my - self. ___

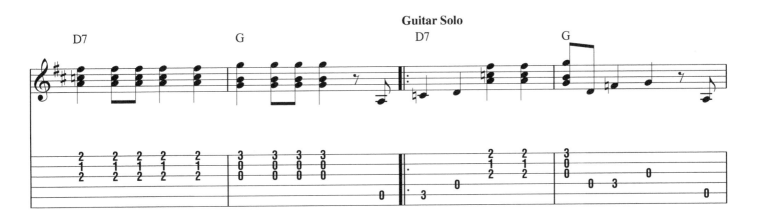

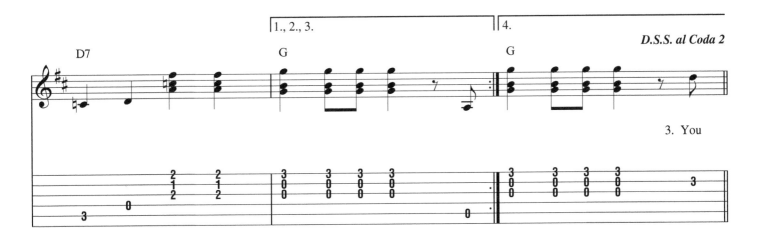

Natural Mystic

Words and Music by Bob Marley

Strum Pattern: 5

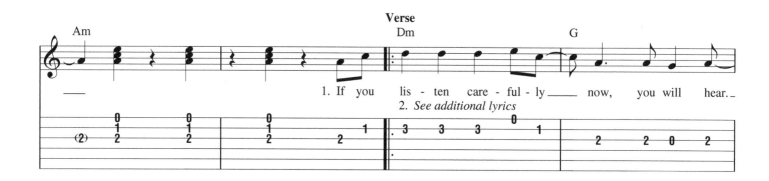

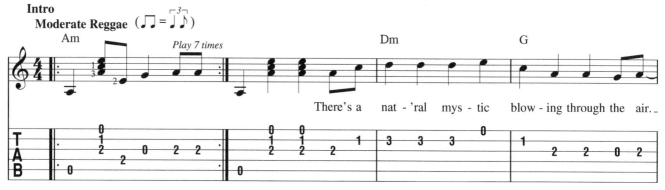

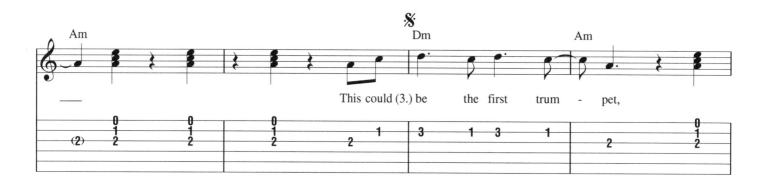

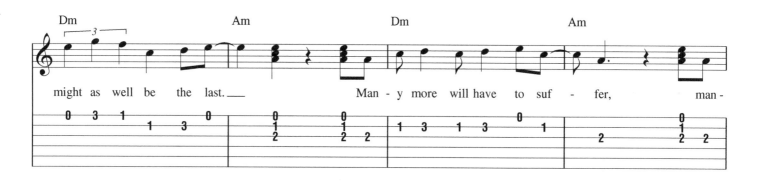

y more will have to die. ___ Don't ask me ___ why.

Chorus

1. Things are not the way ___ they used to be. ___ I won't tell no
2., 3. *See additional lyrics*

To Coda

lie. 2. One If you lis - ten care - ful - ly ___

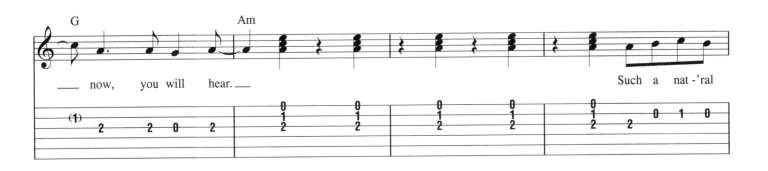

___ now, you will hear. ___ Such a nat -'ral

mys - tic blow - ing through the air.

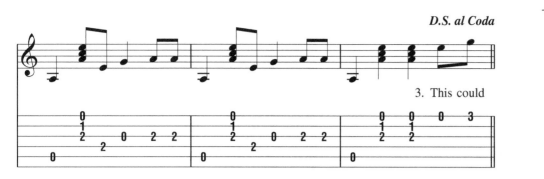

D.S. al Coda

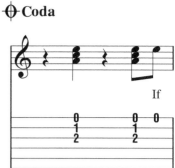

⊕ **Coda**

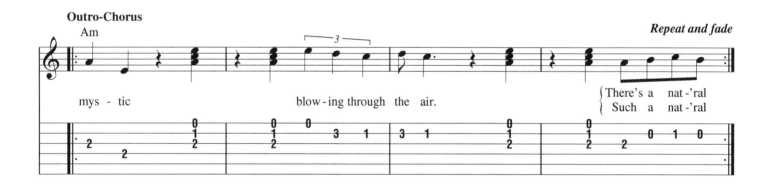

Additional Lyrics

2. One and all got to face reality now.
Though I try to find the answer
To all the questions they ask,
Though I know it's impossible
To go living through the past.
Don't tell no lie.

Chorus 2. There's a nat'ral mystic blowing through the air.
Can't keep them down.
If you listen carefully now, you will hear.
Such a nat'ral mystic blowing through the air.

Chorus 3. There's a nat'ral mystic blowing through the air.
I won't tell no lie.
If you listen carefully now, you will hear.
There's a nat'ral mystic blowing through the air.

No Woman No Cry

Words and Music by Vincent Ford

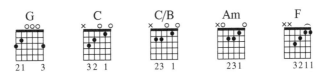

Strum Pattern: 3

Intro

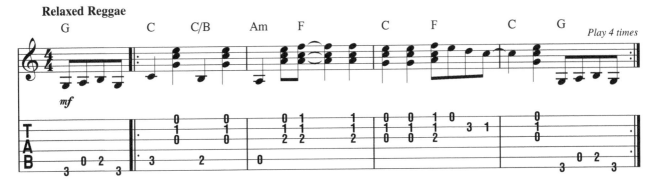

Chorus

No, wom-an, no cry.___   No, wom-an, no cry.___

{ No, wom-an, no cry.
 Here,___ lit-tle dar-lin', don't shed no tears. }   No, wom-an, no cry.___

𝄋 Verse

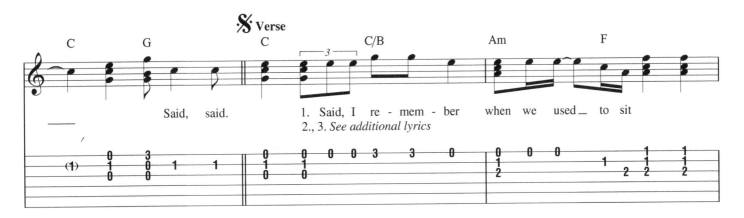

Said, said.   1. Said, I re-mem-ber when we used___ to sit
 2., 3. *See additional lyrics*

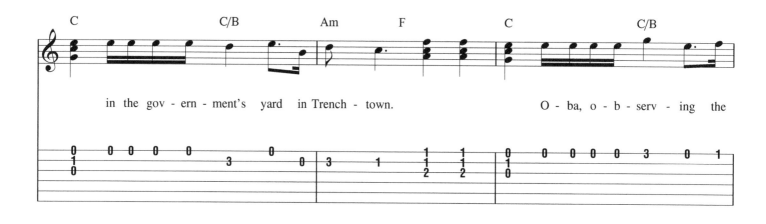

in the gov - ern - ment's yard in Trench - town.   O - ba, o - b - serv - ing the

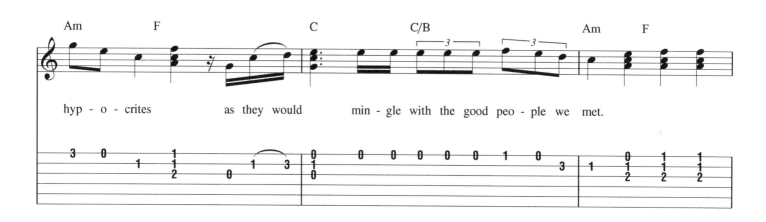

hyp - o - crites   as they would   min - gle with the good peo - ple we met.

Good friends we had,___ oh good friends we've lost___   a - long the way.___

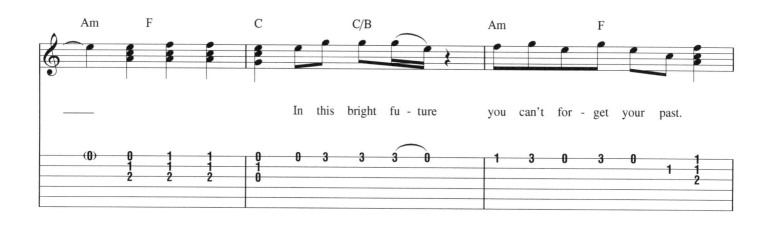

___   In this bright fu - ture   you can't for - get your past.

So, dry your tears___ I ___ say. And ___ through, but while I'm gone, I mean...

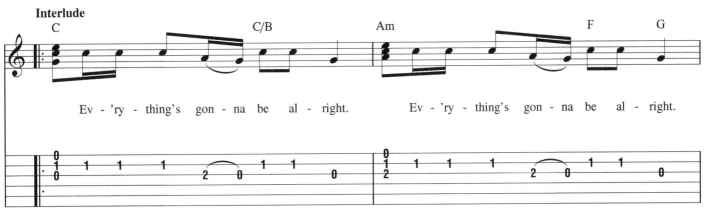

Interlude

Ev - 'ry - thing's gon - na be al - right. Ev - 'ry - thing's gon - na be al - right.

Ev - 'ry-thing's gon - na be al - right. Ev - 'ry-thing's gon - na be al - right.

Chorus

Ev - 'ry - thing's gon - na be al - right. So, wom - an, no cry. No, no

wom-an, no wom-an, no cry.___ Oh, my lit-tle sis-ter, don't shed no tears.___

Guitar Solo

No, wom-an, no cry.___

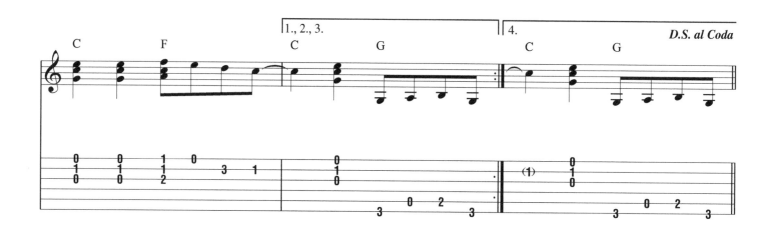

1., 2., 3. | 4. | *D.S. al Coda*

Coda

Chorus

___through, but while I'm gone I mean... No, wom-an, no cry.___

Additional Lyrics

2., 3. Said I remember when we used to sit
In the government's yard in Trenchtown.
And then Georgie would make a firelight
As it was logwood burnin' through the night.
Then we would cook corn meal porridge
Of which I'll share with you.
My feet is my only carriage,
So, I've got to push on through, but while I'm gone I mean...

One Love

Words and Music by Bob Marley

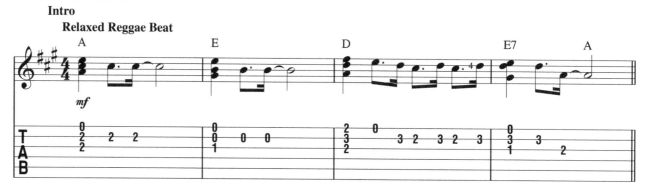

Strum Pattern: 1

Intro

Relaxed Reggae Beat

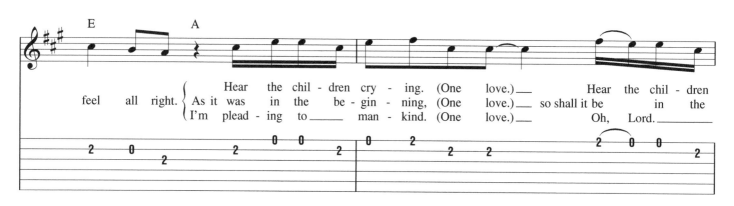

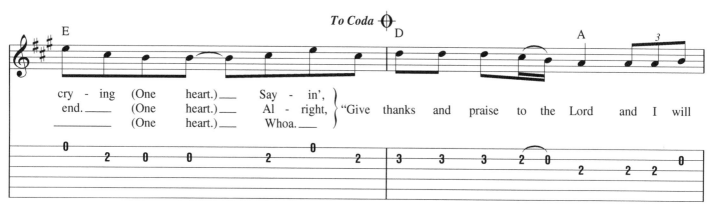

feel all right." Say - in', "Let's get to - geth - er and feel all right." {Whoa, whoa, whoa, whoa. / One more thing.

Verse

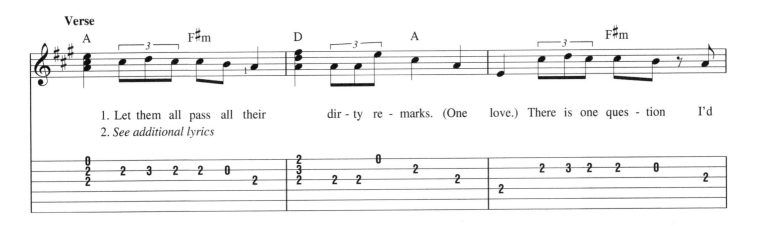

1. Let them all pass all their dir - ty re - marks. (One love.) There is one ques - tion I'd
2. *See additional lyrics*

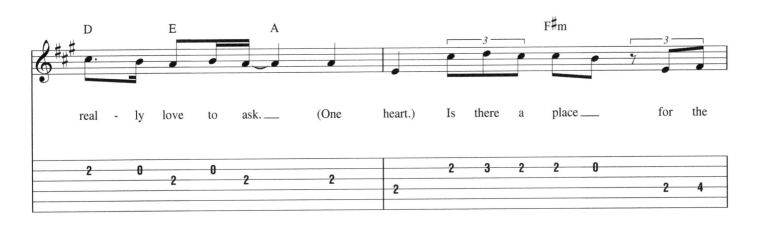

real - ly love to ask. (One heart.) Is there a place for the

hope - less sin - ner who has hurt all man - kind just to

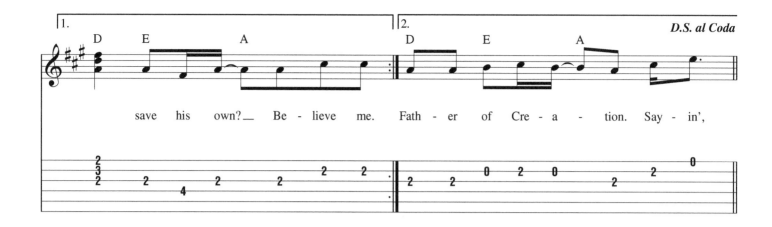

save his own?__ Be - lieve me. Fath - er of Cre - a - tion. Say - in',

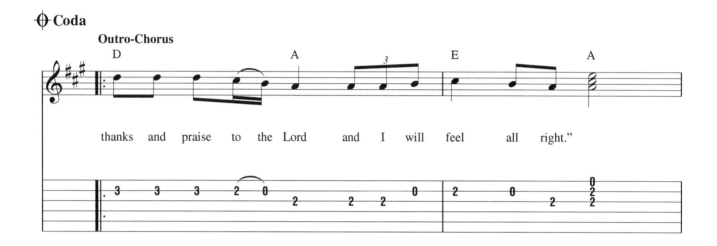

⊕ Coda

Outro-Chorus

thanks and praise to the Lord and I will feel all right."

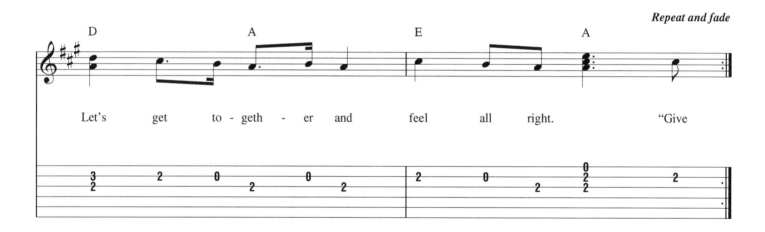

Let's get to - geth - er and feel all right. "Give

Additional Lyrics

2. Let's get together to fight this Holy Armageddon, (One love.)
   So when the man comes there will be no, no doom. (One song.)
   Have pity on those whose chances grow thinner.
   There ain't no hiding place from the Father of Creation.

Who the Cap Fit

Words and Music by Aston Barrett and Carlton Barrett

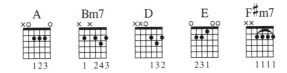

Strum Pattern: 6

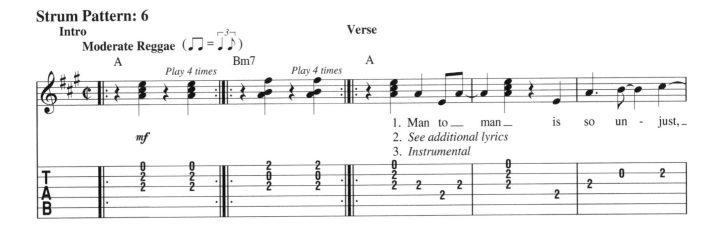

1. Man to __ man __ is so un - just, __
2. *See additional lyrics*
3. *Instrumental*

_____ chil - dren. __ You don't know __ who to trust.

Your worst en - e - my could be your __ best friend, _____ and your

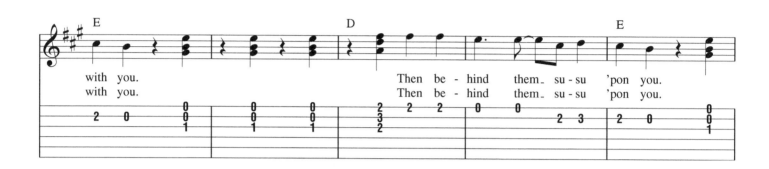

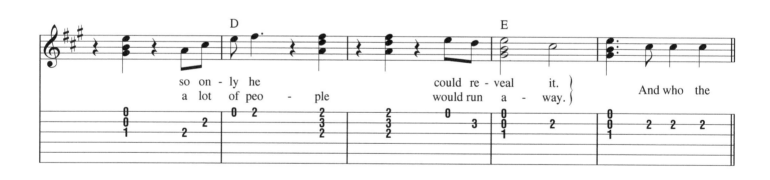

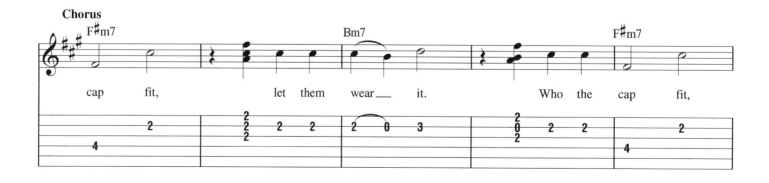

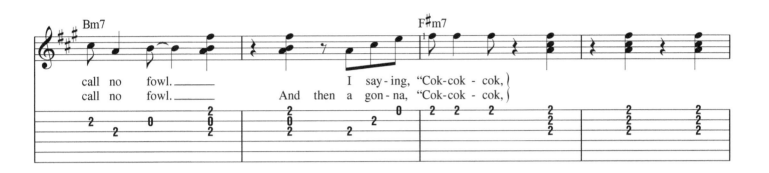

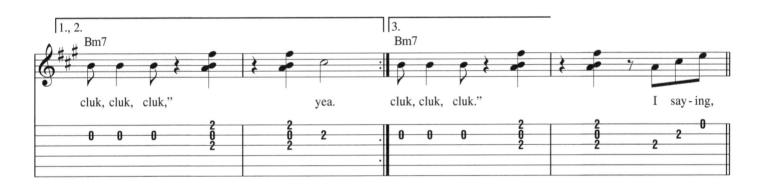

Outro

Repeat and fade

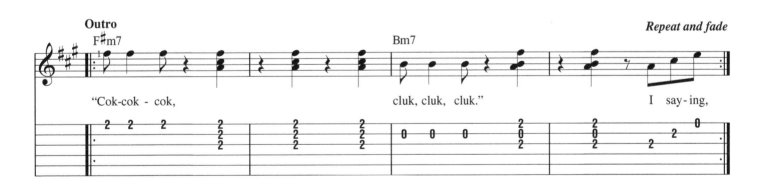

Additional Lyrics

2. Some will hate you, pretend they love you, now.
Then, behind they try to eliminate you.
But who Jah bless, no one curse.
Thank God, we're past the worse.
Hypocrites and parasites
Will come up and take a bite.
And if your night should turn to day,
A lot of people would run away.

So Much Trouble in the World

Words and Music by Bob Marley

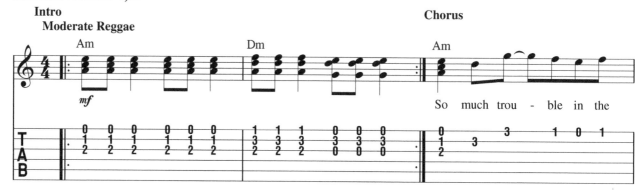

Strum Pattern: 1, 5

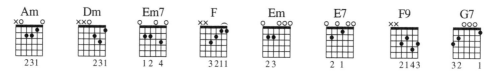

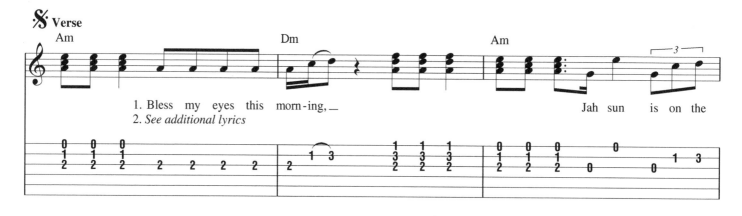

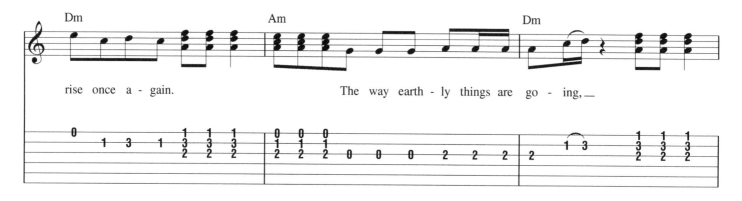

an - y - thing can hap - pen. You see____ men sail - ing on their e - go trips,

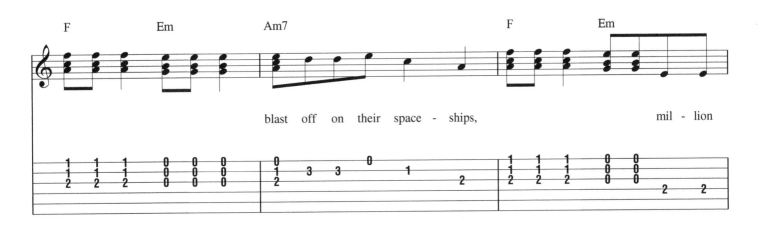

blast off on their space - ships,   mil - lion

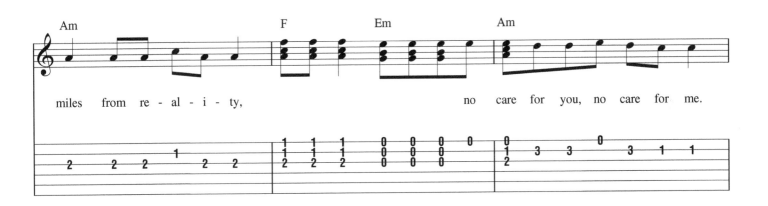

miles from re - al - i - ty,   no care for you, no care for me.

To Coda ⊕

Chorus

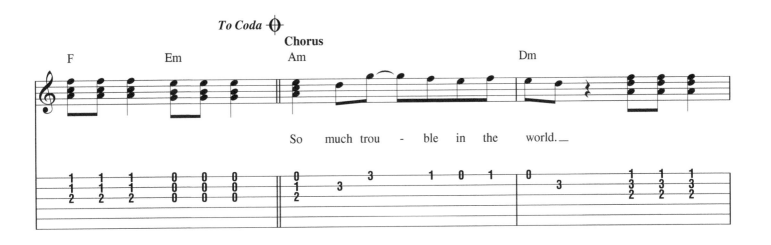

So much trou - ble in the world.____

So much trou - ble in the world. ___ All you got to do is

give a lit - tle, take a lit - tle, give a lit - tle one more time.

Give a lit - tle, take a lit - tle, give a lit - tle.

Bridge

So you think you found the so - lu - tion.

But it's just an - oth - er il - lu - sion.

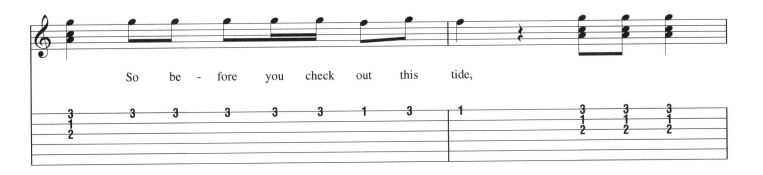

So be-fore you check out this tide,

D.S. al Coda

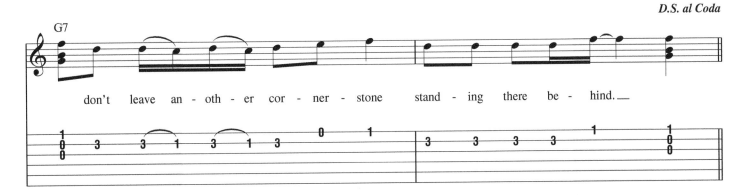

G7

don't leave an-oth-er cor-ner-stone stand-ing there be-hind.

⊕ Coda
Outro-Chorus

Am   Dm

{ So }
{ so } much trou-ble in the world. ___

Repeat and fade

Am   Dm

So much trou-ble in the world. ___   There is

Additional Lyrics

2. We've got to face the day.
   Ooh wee, come that may.
   We the street people talking.
   We the people struggling.
   Now, they're sitting on a time bomb.
   Now I know the time has come.
   What goes on up is coming on down.
   Goes around and comes around.

Stir It Up

Words and Music by Bob Marley

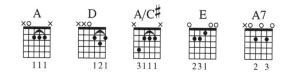

Strum Pattern: 2

Intro

Moderate Reggae

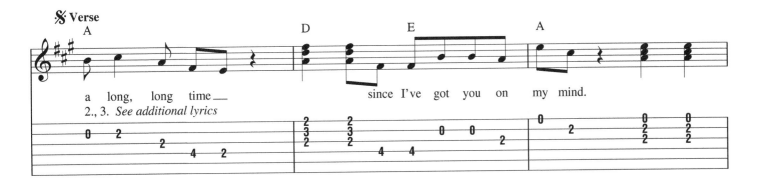

a long, long time ___ since I've got you on my mind.
2., 3. *See additional lyrics*

And now you are ___ here, I say it's so clear. ___

See what we can do, ba-by, just me and you. Come on and is keep it in. { And } { So }

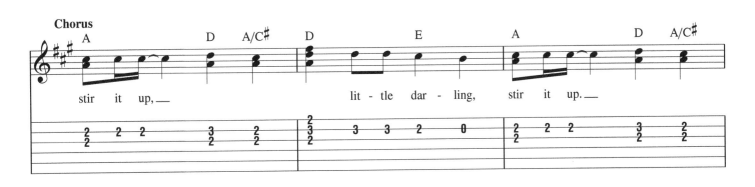

stir it up, ___ lit-tle dar-ling, stir it up. ___

Come on and stir it up, ___ ooh, lit - tle dar - ling,

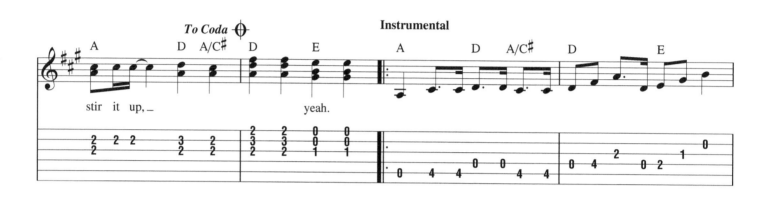

To Coda ⊕   **Instrumental**

stir it up, ___ yeah.

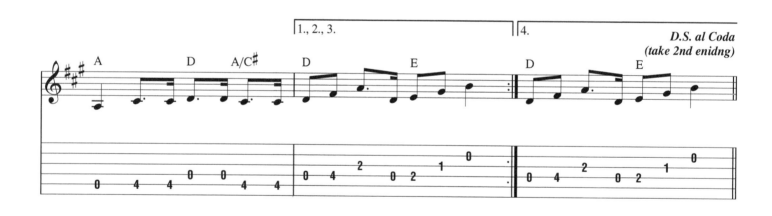

|1., 2., 3. |4.   *D.S. al Coda*
(take 2nd enidng)

⊕ **Coda**

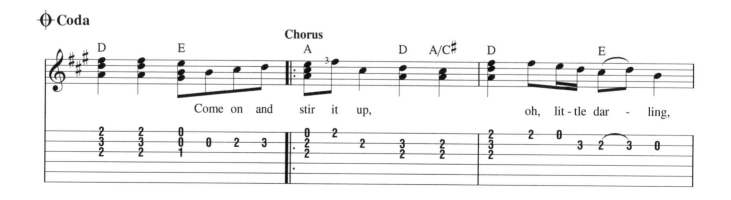

Chorus

Come on and stir it up, oh, lit - tle dar - ling,

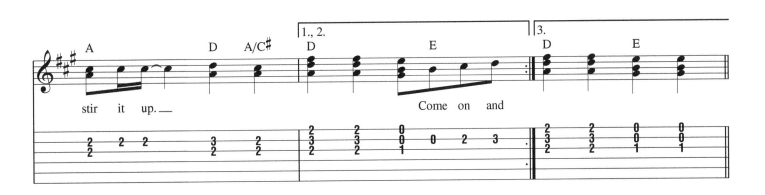

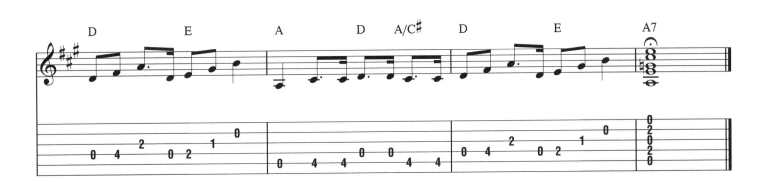

Additional Lyrics

2. I'll push the wood, I'll blaze your fire,
   Then I'll satisfy your, your heart's desire.
   Said I'll stir it, yeah, ev'ry minute, yeah.
   All you got to do, baby, is keep it in.

3. Oh, will you quench me while I'm thirsty?
   Or would you cool me down when I'm hot?
   Your recipe, darling, is so tasty,
   And you sure can stir your pot.

Three Little Birds

Words and Music by Bob Marley

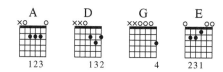

Strum Pattern: 2

Intro
Moderately slow

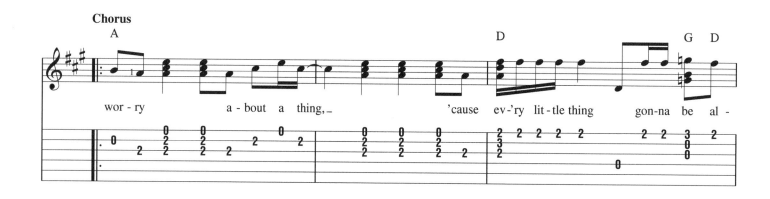

wor - ry   a - bout a thing, __   'cause ev -'ry lit - tle thing   gon - na be al -

right.   Sing - in', don't wor - ry   a - bout a thing, __   'cause

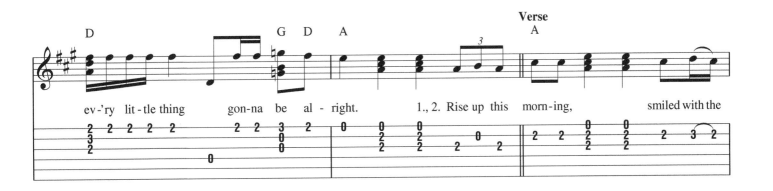

ev-'ry lit-tle thing gon-na be al-right. 1., 2. Rise up this morn-ing, smiled with the

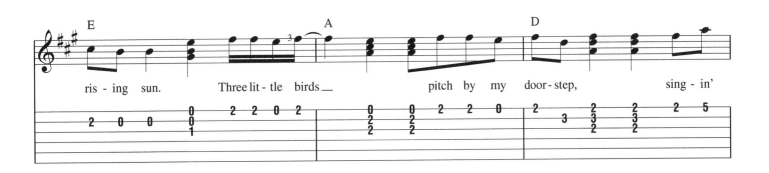

ris-ing sun. Three lit-tle birds ___ pitch by my door-step, sing-in'

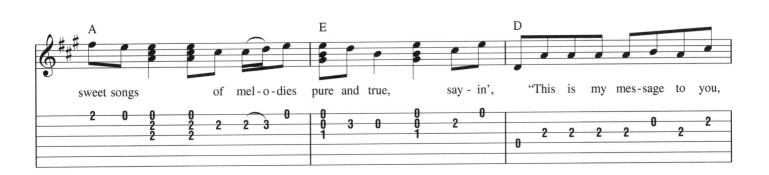

sweet songs of mel-o-dies pure and true, say-in', "This is my mes-sage to you,

1.
whoo, hoo." Sing-in', don't whoo, hoo." 2. Sing-in', don't wor-ry a-bout a thing,___

Outro-Chorus

Repeat and fade

___ 'cause ev-'ry lit-tle thing gon-na be al-right. Sing-in', don't

Time Will Tell

Words and Music by Bob Marley

Strum Pattern: 1

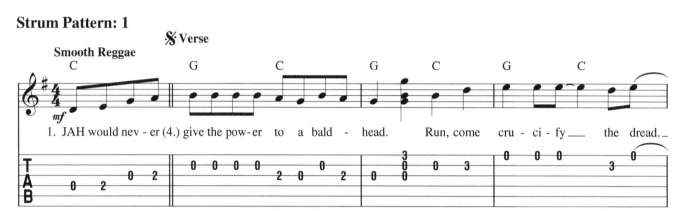

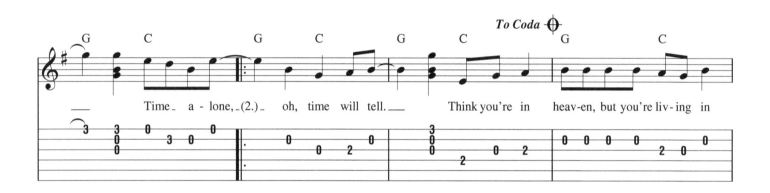

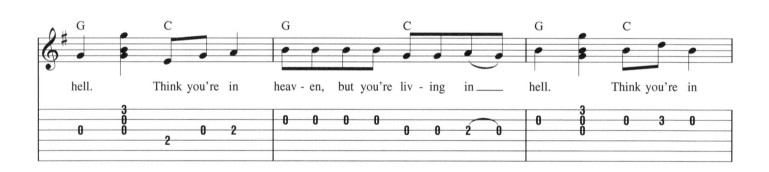

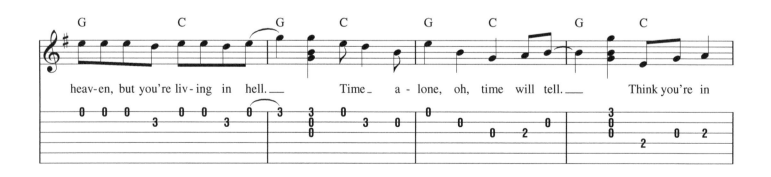

Turn Your Lights Down Low

Words and Music by Bob Marley

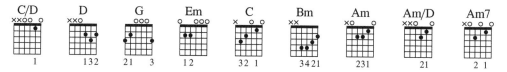

Strum Pattern: 1

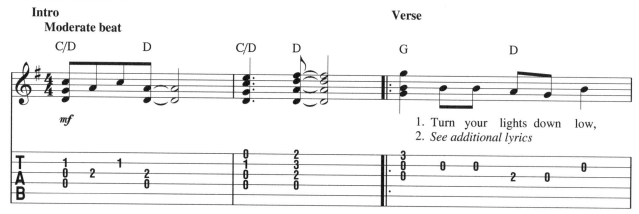

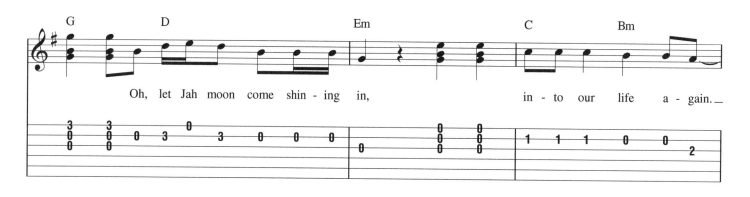

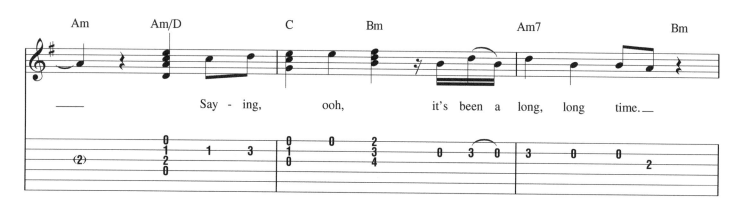

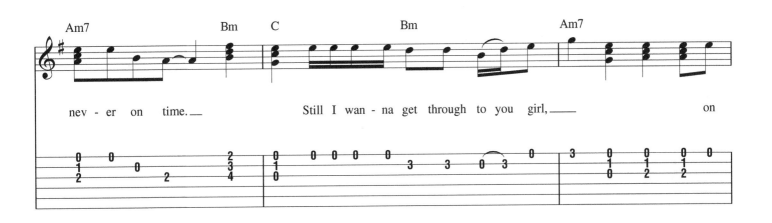

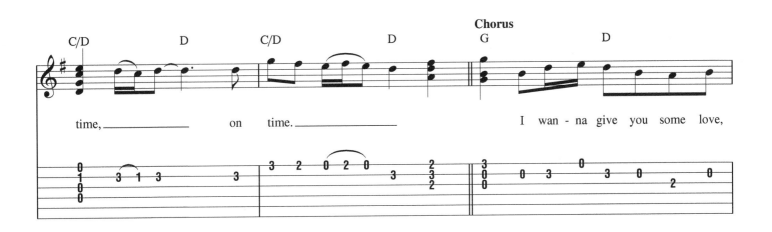

Chorus

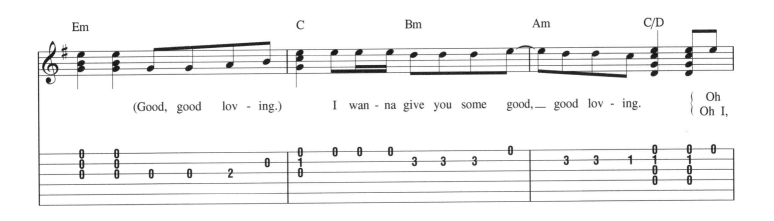

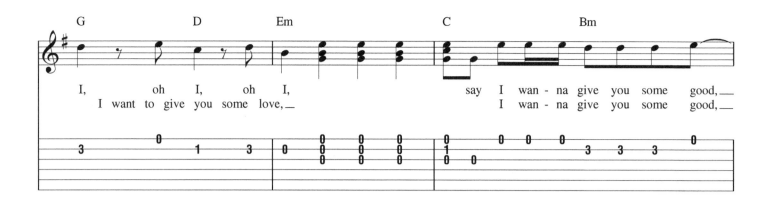

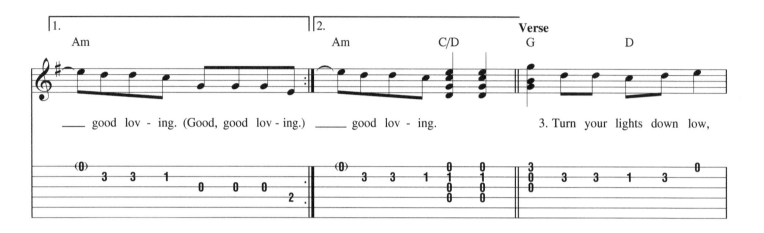

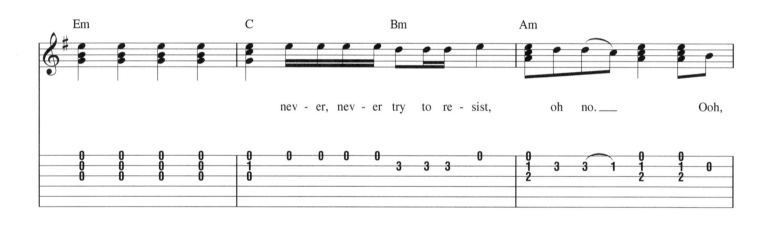

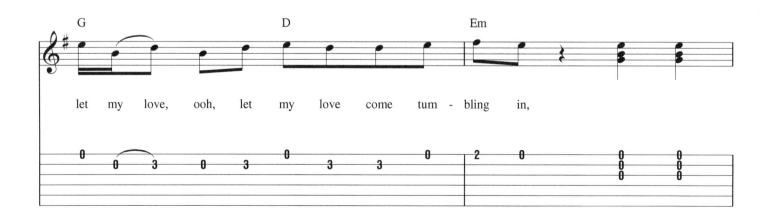

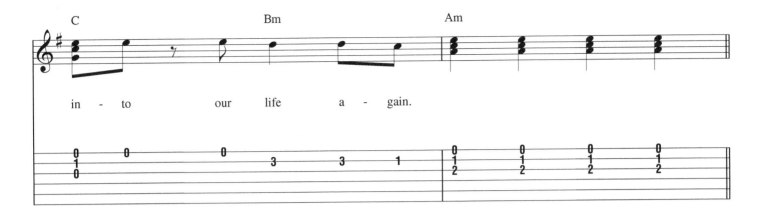

into our life a - gain.

Outro-Chorus

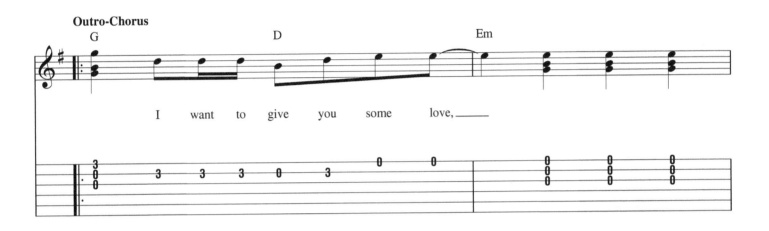

I want to give you some love, ____

Repeat and fade

I want to give you some good, ____ good lov - ing.

Additional Lyrics

2. Turn your lights down low,
   Never try to resist, oh, no.
   Oh, let my love come tumbling in
   Into our life again.
   Saying, ooh, I love you
   And I want you to know right now.
   Ooh, I love you
   And I want you to know right now.
   'Cause I, that I...

Waiting in Vain

Words and Music by Bob Marley

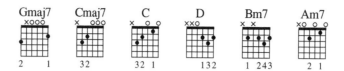

Strum Pattern: 7

Intro

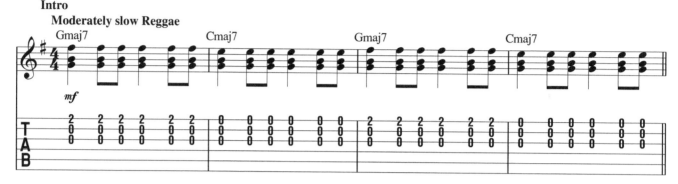

Chorus

I don't wan-na wait — in vain — for your love. — I don't wan-na wait — in vain —

%. Verse

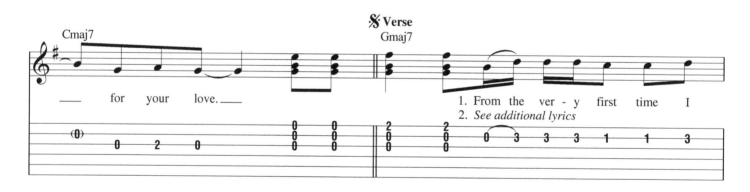

— for your love. —
1. From the ver-y first time I
2. *See additional lyrics*

blessed my eyes on you, — girl, my heart says, "Fol-low through."

But I know now that I'm way down on your line, but the wait-ing feel is

fine. So don't treat me like a pup-pet on a string,

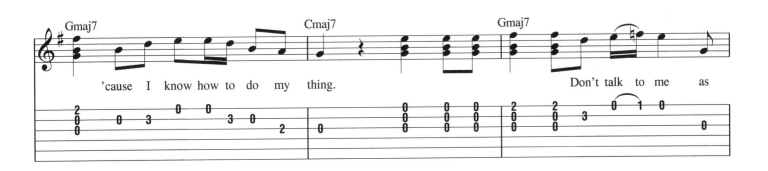

'cause I know how to do my thing. Don't talk to me as

if you think I'm dumb. I wan-na know when you're gon-na come. See,

Chorus

I don't wan-na wait in vain for your love. I don't wan-na wait in vain

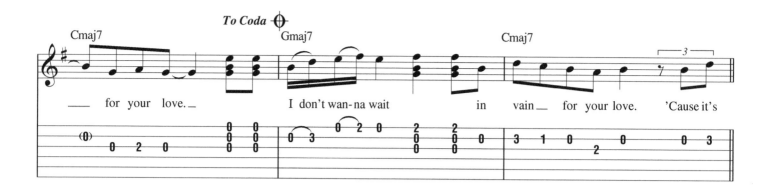

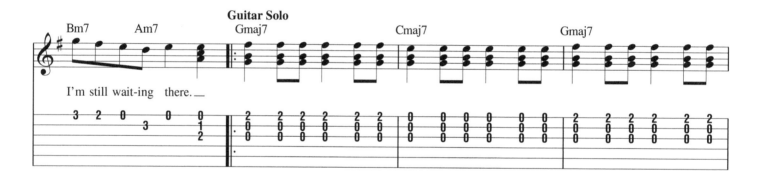

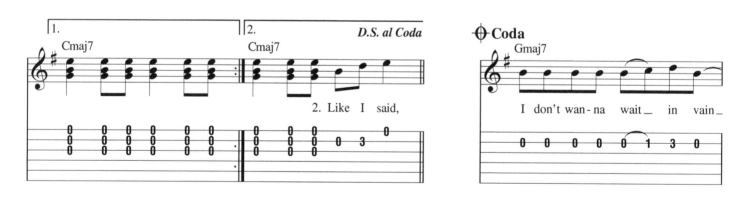

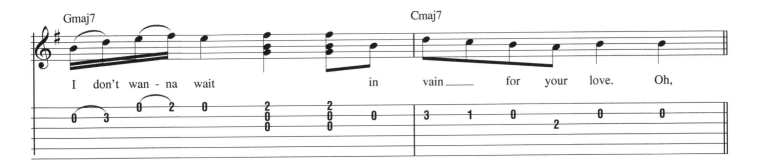

Outro

Repeat and fade

Additional Lyrics

2. It's been three years since I'm knockin' on your door,
And still can knock some more.
Ooh girl, ooh girl, is it feasible,
I wanna know now, for I to knock some more?
Ya see, in life I know there's lots of grief,
But your love is my relief.
Tears in my eyes burn, tears in my eyes burn
While I'm waiting, while I'm waiting for my turn.

EASY GUITAR
WITH NOTES & TAB

This series features simplified arrangements with notes, tab, chord charts, and strum and pick patterns.

MIXED FOLIOS

00702287	Acoustic	$19.99
00702002	Acoustic Rock Hits for Easy Guitar	$15.99
00702166	All-Time Best Guitar Collection	$19.99
00702232	Best Acoustic Songs for Easy Guitar	$16.99
00119835	Best Children's Songs	$16.99
00703055	The Big Book of Nursery Rhymes & Children's Songs	$16.99
00698978	Big Christmas Collection	$19.99
00702394	Bluegrass Songs for Easy Guitar	$15.99
00289632	Bohemian Rhapsody	$19.99
00703387	Celtic Classics	$14.99
00224808	Chart Hits of 2016-2017	$14.99
00267383	Chart Hits of 2017-2018	$14.99
00334293	Chart Hits of 2019-2020	$16.99
00702149	Children's Christian Songbook	$9.99
00702028	Christmas Classics	$8.99
00101779	Christmas Guitar	$14.99
00702141	Classic Rock	$8.95
00159642	Classical Melodies	$12.99
00253933	Disney/Pixar's Coco	$16.99
00702203	CMT's 100 Greatest Country Songs	$34.99
00702283	The Contemporary Christian Collection	$16.99
00196954	Contemporary Disney	$19.99
00702239	Country Classics for Easy Guitar	$24.99

00702257	Easy Acoustic Guitar Songs	$16.99
00702041	Favorite Hymns for Easy Guitar	$12.99
00222701	Folk Pop Songs	$17.99
00126894	Frozen	$14.99
00333922	Frozen 2	$14.99
00702286	Glee	$16.99
00702160	The Great American Country Songbook	$19.99
00702148	Great American Gospel for Guitar	$14.99
00702050	Great Classical Themes for Easy Guitar	$9.99
00275088	The Greatest Showman	$17.99
00148030	Halloween Guitar Songs	$14.99
00702273	Irish Songs	$12.99
00192503	Jazz Classics for Easy Guitar	$16.99
00702275	Jazz Favorites for Easy Guitar	$17.99
00702274	Jazz Standards for Easy Guitar	$19.99
00702162	Jumbo Easy Guitar Songbook	$24.99
00232285	La La Land	$16.99
00702258	Legends of Rock	$14.99
00702189	MTV's 100 Greatest Pop Songs	$34.99
00702272	1950s Rock	$16.99
00702271	1960s Rock	$16.99
00702270	1970s Rock	$19.99
00702269	1980s Rock	$15.99
00702268	1990s Rock	$19.99
00369043	Rock Songs for Kids	$14.99

00109725	Once	$14.99
00702187	Selections from O Brother Where Art Thou?	$19.99
00702178	100 Songs for Kids	$14.99
00702515	Pirates of the Caribbean	$17.99
00702125	Praise and Worship for Guitar	$14.99
00287930	Songs from A Star Is Born, The Greatest Showman, La La Land, and More Movie Musicals	$16.99
00702285	Southern Rock Hits	$12.99
00156420	Star Wars Music	$16.99
00121535	30 Easy Celtic Guitar Solos	$16.99
00702156	3-Chord Rock	$12.99
00244654	Top Hits of 2017	$14.99
00283786	Top Hits of 2018	$14.99
00702294	Top Worship Hits	$17.99
00702255	VH1's 100 Greatest Hard Rock Songs	$34.99
00702175	VH1's 100 Greatest Songs of Rock and Roll	$29.99
00702253	Wicked	$12.99

ARTIST COLLECTIONS

00702267	AC/DC for Easy Guitar	$16.99
00702598	Adele for Easy Guitar	$15.99
00156221	Adele – 25	$16.99
00702040	Best of the Allman Brothers	$16.99
00702865	J.S. Bach for Easy Guitar	$15.99
00702169	Best of The Beach Boys	$15.99
00702292	The Beatles — 1	$22.99
00125796	Best of Chuck Berry	$15.99
00702201	The Essential Black Sabbath	$15.99
00702250	blink-182 — Greatest Hits	$17.99
02501615	Zac Brown Band — The Foundation	$17.99
02501621	Zac Brown Band — You Get What You Give	$16.99
00702043	Best of Johnny Cash	$17.99
00702090	Eric Clapton's Best	$16.99
00702086	Eric Clapton — from the Album Unplugged	$17.99
00702202	The Essential Eric Clapton	$17.99
00702053	Best of Patsy Cline	$15.99
00222697	Very Best of Coldplay – 2nd Edition	$16.99
00702229	The Very Best of Creedence Clearwater Revival	$16.99
00702145	Best of Jim Croce	$16.99
00702278	Crosby, Stills & Nash	$12.99
14042809	Bob Dylan	$15.99
00702276	Fleetwood Mac — Easy Guitar Collection	$17.99
00139462	The Very Best of Grateful Dead	$16.99
00702136	Best of Merle Haggard	$16.99
00702227	Jimi Hendrix — Smash Hits	$19.99
00702288	Best of Hillsong United	$12.99
00702236	Best of Antonio Carlos Jobim	$15.99
00702245	Elton John — Greatest Hits 1970–2002	$19.99

00129855	Jack Johnson	$16.99
00702204	Robert Johnson	$14.99
00702234	Selections from Toby Keith — 35 Biggest Hits	$12.95
00702003	Kiss	$16.99
00702216	Lynyrd Skynyrd	$16.99
00702182	The Essential Bob Marley	$16.99
00146081	Maroon 5	$14.99
00121925	Bruno Mars – Unorthodox Jukebox	$12.99
00702248	Paul McCartney — All the Best	$14.99
00125484	The Best of MercyMe	$12.99
00702209	Steve Miller Band — Young Hearts (Greatest Hits)	$12.95
00124167	Jason Mraz	$15.99
00702096	Best of Nirvana	$16.99
00702211	The Offspring — Greatest Hits	$17.99
00138026	One Direction	$17.99
00702030	Best of Roy Orbison	$17.99
00702144	Best of Ozzy Osbourne	$14.99
00702279	Tom Petty	$17.99
00102911	Pink Floyd	$17.99
00702139	Elvis Country Favorites	$19.99
00702293	The Very Best of Prince	$19.99
00699415	Best of Queen for Guitar	$16.99
00109279	Best of R.E.M.	$14.99
00702208	Red Hot Chili Peppers — Greatest Hits	$16.99
00198960	The Rolling Stones	$17.99
00174793	The Very Best of Santana	$16.99
00702196	Best of Bob Seger	$16.99
00146046	Ed Sheeran	$15.99
00702252	Frank Sinatra — Nothing But the Best	$12.99
00702010	Best of Rod Stewart	$17.99
00702049	Best of George Strait	$17.99

00702259	Taylor Swift for Easy Guitar	$15.99
00359800	Taylor Swift – Easy Guitar Anthology	$24.99
00702260	Taylor Swift — Fearless	$14.99
00139727	Taylor Swift — 1989	$17.99
00115960	Taylor Swift — Red	$16.99
00253667	Taylor Swift — Reputation	$17.99
00702290	Taylor Swift — Speak Now	$16.99
00232849	Chris Tomlin Collection – 2nd Edition	$14.99
00702226	Chris Tomlin — See the Morning	$12.95
00148643	Train	$14.99
00702427	U2 — 18 Singles	$19.99
00702108	Best of Stevie Ray Vaughan	$17.99
00279005	The Who	$14.99
00702123	Best of Hank Williams	$15.99
00194548	Best of John Williams	$14.99
00702228	Neil Young — Greatest Hits	$17.99
00119133	Neil Young — Harvest	$14.99

Prices, contents and availability subject to change without notice.

HAL•LEONARD®

Visit Hal Leonard online at **halleonard.com**